We All Go Together

The Loving Light Books Series

Also by Liane Rich

Loving Light

Book 7

We All Go Together

Liane Rich

The information contained in this book is not intended as a substitute for professional medical advice. Neither the publisher nor the author is engaged in rendering professional advice to the reader. The remedies and suggestions in this book should not be taken, or construed, as standard medical diagnosis, prescription or treatment. For any medical issue or illness consult a qualified physician.

Loving Light Books
Original Copyright © 1992
Copyright © 2009 Liane

ISBN 13: 978-1-878480-07-1
ISBN 10: 1-878480-07-3

Loving Light Books:
www.lovinglightbooks.com

Also Available at:
Amazon: www.amazon.com
Barnes & Noble: www.barnesandnoble.com

for John F.

The information in this series is not necessarily meant to be taken literally. It is meant to *shift* your consciousness....

Foreword

Anyone immersed in the vast body of new metaphysical knowledge is aware of the virtual symphony of voices from channeled sources throughout the world – inspirational voices that may be artistic, poetic, philosophical, religious, or scientific. And now, out of these myriad New Age voices, comes a series of books by God, channeled through Liane, revealing the frank truth in all its glory and wonder, telling us how to cleanse our bodies, gain access to our subconscious minds, clear our other selves and march back to who we are – God.

In God's books you will be introduced to a loving, powerful, gripping, exciting, and often humorous voice that reaches out and speaks ever so personally to the individual reader. As the reader's interest deepens, invariably an intimate relationship to this voice develops. It is a relationship that lasts forever, and I am quite certain I do mean forever.

Here is an accelerated program, a no-holds-barred course, where God guides us and loves us, and as needs be recommends books to us and even a movie or musical piece along the way. He (She) enters our lives and sees through our eyes, seeming to enjoy the ride as He guides us back to US, back to ALL. Here is a voice that is playful and informative, that is humorous and serious, that is gentle and powerfully divine. It is a voice that knows no barriers or restrictions, a straightforward and honest voice that caresses us when we need the warmth and pushes us when we are immobilized.

In today's New Age literature there is an avalanche of information from magnificent beings of light, information that possesses us and compels us to look at our fears and express our love. In this series of books by God, you will find truly powerful methods for making this transition from toxicity to purity, from density to light, from fear to love, and from the delusion of death to the awakening to full life. You will experience in these books the love and the power of God for it is your love to express and your power to behold. Rarely will you see more lucid steps for transformation. Read these beautiful words and rejoice in our period of awakening, our return to Home.

John Farrell, PhD., LCSW. – Psychologist, Clinical Social Worker, Senior Clinician Psychiatric Emergency Services, U.C. Davis Medical Center, Sacramento. John is also a retired Professor – California State University, Sacramento, in Health Sciences and Psychology.

We All Go Together

Introduction

*S*o far no one believes that I am who I say. However, most of you believe that I am most unusual and even informative. My greatest challenge has been "entering form." Matter is so *dense* that it is quite difficult to take part in your lives. So; why doesn't God communicate with everyone on earth and why now? These and other questions will be addressed in this, our seventh book of this "Loving Light" series.

Most of you are so far *into* density that you are as solid as granite! You "feel" human and you look human, but you are not. You are so dense that you can no longer vibrate at a good enough speed to save yourselves. You have slowed down and stood still to the point of decay. You no longer spin and vibrate so you no longer live. In the same way that a candle burns itself out by burying itself in its own wax, you bury yourself in your own density and extinguish – no more light, no more love, no more lovelight.

Let your lovelight burn. Go out and forgive all those you hold grievance toward, for they are simply those you asked to help you "see" through this dense field to who you really are. They will allow you to spin-out in a new direction. In forgiving your debtors you "perceive" your world differently, and in perceiving it as forgiveness you begin to *receive* forgiveness. Forgiveness from whom? – you ask. From you. You are holding so many judgments against who and what you are that I could not begin to convince you that "you are God." You got flooded by your own wax! Your wick is still in place, however your light has gone out and we must now dig around you to find you and re-ignite your life force. Life force is leaving body rapidly and that is why you see so much death at this time. Souls are getting out whenever and wherever they can.

My biggest problem has been "entering" this dense field. In order to channel this information, I must hook up quite a connection in order to keep Liane safe and unharmed by my vibration as well as the "*intent*" that circles this plane. Intent says, "No, you do not believe you are God." And intent says "No, you do not access God," and intent also tries to stop God from entering matter. Intent is simply you. *You* intend to stay blind to the fact that God *is* you in all your glory and even your humility. You *are* this information. You have created a force field to keep you from knowing and now this field has been penetrated by God; and there are many who will not wish to know that "God has come to earth." This Second Coming is not so dramatic as the first, but you get the idea.

So; God is now on earth and I am not being shut down or censored in any way. Liane takes her job as pen seriously and she has undergone many changes in order to stay with me, so to speak. Actually it is more to the point to say she stays tuned to my vibration. Most of which is done by going into and facing her fear. Fear is simply a very dense form of you. You are the only one here and yet you pretend you are not God and you pretend you are not Satan. *You are everything that exists.* There is nothing more. It is *all* you and you are all of everything.

࿓

*H*ow do you like being God? Most often you are so "caught" up in living *in* matter that you rarely know anything about *you*. You are not simply the human self. You go to seminars and learn to meditate so that you might raise your level of vibration to some extent. The only problem with meditation at this time is its inability to clear density in order to vibrate while in a conscious relaxed state, as well as when in an altered state of consciousness. Most often you are being programmed (while in meditation) to go deeper *into* matter.

Matter is not bad nor is it evil. Matter *is.* Now; most of you want more! You want more money, more love and more fun. You want more happiness and even more sex. Most of you are in a constant state of wanting. This is how you get more: You begin to vibrate "out" of matter and you no longer will want more, as you will *have* it all. More is simply a state of mind and when I can convince you of this, I will have you back on track. To *get* – give! When you give you tell the universe that you have more than enough and so this universe (which is yours to begin with… created by you through your belief patterns) begins to give you *more*, because you are creating a "more" than enough program.

Now, for those who do "not have," I wish you to know that "to give" is not only matter, it is also spirit and it is energy. Give what you have. Christ taught his followers to give away their belongings because he knew how it would enrich their lives and quell their fears about not having. Most of you "feel" poor or at least "not rich." Those who do feel "not rich" hold on to every possession as though it will never be replaced if lost or stolen.

This is a poverty created mentality. You must break through this belief system in some way before you will begin to see results in the prosperity circle. Yes, prosperity is a circle and it flows endlessly and returns again and again to its sender. Poverty is also a circle and it returns again and again to its sender. Get off the poverty line and onto the prosperity line. Poverty does not run through you as it is too dense. It runs around you and blocks your every move. Prosperity, on the other hand, does flow through you and back out to increase and divide and begin to come back to you in other areas.

Now; when you begin to prosper you will wish

to continue to give. This is not a mandatory ten percent as taught by so many. To give is to love. If you love to paint, you *give* to the entire world by the joy you express outward as you create. Your work may never make it on display or even in the market place but your "reward" will return in the form of energy. Energy put out is energy received. Now; when you begin to put out energy that is powerful and says, "I am happy and in love with myself," you will "receive" the best of both worlds.

Love of self is not high on many priority lists so far. Self-esteem and self-gratification seem to meet and merge and are now fed by addictive, compulsive behavior. The more you spend on you the better you feel. An expensive car tells you that you are okay and so you believe the programming of your commercials. You do not "consciously" realize how programmed you are. To strip you bare of all possessions would leave you devastated and hurt, and some of you would "feel" so bad and under-privileged that you might kill yourself, because you cannot live in poverty and plow the land and raise food and grow vegetables for market. You have come too far, and to go back would be offensive and undermining to your character.

So now you have it… *you* believe yourself to be only as valuable as your toys. You who live in splendor *are* splendid. Those who live in squalor are squalid and those who live on the road with no hopes of settling down somewhere are considered nomads with no one to love. You are so wrong in your thinking. You travel and sightsee and dine and carry on like material wealth is all that is important. You got so caught up in money and power that you forgot that *you* are power. You hold the world in your hands because *you* are this entire universe. You do not create out of love, you create out of fear that you will die. It is that simple. When you were young you didn't care. It was programmed into you that you must be productive and strive for perfection, or you will become a "nobody" – a nothing. I am here to say that *you* are the entire world.

You, without your hang-ups and neurosis and fears and letdowns and uncomfortable-ness, are just about perfection as you are. You are not dumb. You are not slow. You are not stupid. You are not out of sync; you are simply misprogrammed. You were told how you must be in order to be accepted by the rest of your peers. Now you are so bogged down with misinformation that I have a great mess to "clear" up.

You will begin to realize how you are not what others believe you to be, and in doing so, you will begin to do for you and not out of fear of being different or strange. You are each unique in that you each "hold" information within your cellular structure that is individualized. This information is contained in all areas of matter and when you *wake up* you will see how you fit into God's body. Each and every cell in God's body has a job to do, and once we get you cleared of density and debris you will be running smoothly and right on track.

So for now, I suggest that you begin to love you and stop trying to show everyone else how spectacular you can be. When you truly love the self there is no need to produce results to *show* your wonderfulness. I expect you to continue to read my books and I expect you to continue to visualize your own God-self. You are the only one here....

≈⅏≈

Now; I wish to discuss rape. Most often you are shocked and appalled when rape is instigated by a member of your family or even your community. Most often you see rape as violent, brutal and even sadistic. I want to give you a new *view* on this age old problem. Yes, I said "age old." It has existed for hundreds and even thousands of your earth years. It is nothing new and it is nothing to fear.

Why do you fear rape? Mostly because you put so much emphasis on your own body and how you use it for your own gratification. You do not use your body for sex as often as you could. Most of you are so afraid of this sexual energy that you feel "out of control" or led around by your sex organs. You either stifle sex or you go crazy for sex. So far there is *no* balance. Programming has begun to interfere in all areas of your life. *Sex is not bad.* Nothing on earth is bad. It is only *how* you view it.

So; sex was thought to have power. Why? Because a man could control his woman by suggesting he hold her or cuddle her and she melted into his arms. Why? She "needs" affection to survive. Why? She is intuition and intuition survives through contact with the rest of God's body. Who is God's body... right! All of you. So why does man not need this affection and cuddliness to survive? Man is progressive energy and he builds his own reserves and he is independent of woman. He can survive more easily in the jungle and he protects woman because she falls apart when threatened by big danger. And why does she fall apart? She has been told that she is feminine and this is the role she must play.

She believes what she has been told and now we see woman giving sex to man in order to get shelter and food. This system is not bad. You created it to survive. Man protects woman who is the bearer of children. The woman repays man by giving him love and sex and caring. Love and caring have not been abused, so what went wrong with sex?

Mostly it is a matter of "great" guilt. Sex has been taught and used as a weapon to get what you want. Women have used sex to get what they want and men have used it to get their way. Most of you still use sex. You may not call it sex, but you try to seduce your boss into believing you are great and you seduce others into believing only the best about you. This is good. Who ever said that seduction is wrong? Who ever said that *sex* is wrong? Oh, now we're getting somewhere. So; sex is to be used for baby making and nothing more. Where did this one come from?

I will explain. Once you were so afraid of your own sexual power that you shut down sex to save yourself from your own fear of your own body energies. Sex is simply a powerful movement of energy within the body. It is expressed outwardly in body movement. You flow with sex and often get so caught up in it that you "channel" it through you in the same way that Liane "channels" my energy. You rock and quake and perspire and climax, and it is so wonderful to see that kind of "life force" energy. Move it, use it and do not abuse it.

Do not believe that it controls you. You are always in the driver's seat when you decide to be. Don't let sex give you a ride. Begin to enjoy sex and flow with it. It is not to be judged as undesirable and it is not unlawful and it is not harmful. There would never be trauma behind sexual intercourse if there were not judgment somewhere against it. How do you think it feels to be God and watch you go so haywire over the simplest body process?

You've lost touch with your true self. You are programmed to believe that sexual assault is the most harmful psychologically and emotionally. Stop looking at situations as horrible and they will cease to be so horror filled. You are making situations tragic by your own belief in tragedy. You *need* more and more fear because you contain so much fear. And what you are is what you get, and when you see through love the world gives love. When you see through fear the world gives fear right back. You always get just what you expect, so I suggest that you start "expecting" good and giving "good" thought to every situation… even rape.

We will discuss this further as Liane is in pain from this session and I must allow her to rest.

You do not realize the extent of your humor. Most often you get very stressed out and burdened by what you see and what you hear. Can you imagine how it would be to not be affected by what you call bad news, or what society classifies as horror? It is not how you see it that gets you upset. It is how you allow it to be so awful that creates problems for you. Can you imagine just walking to work whistling a tune and someone comes up with a gun and says, "Give me your cash and jewelry." You panic and get frightened and hand over the goods. You go on to your work place and inform your fellow employees as well as your boss that you are the victim of a robbery. So now the entire office is buzzing with the news and excitement, and you are getting sympathy and comfort and it makes you feel better.

Mostly you just want your money back and, of course, your jewelry which is very expensive and shows everyone your status. You love that jewelry and *always* wear it because it is your favorite piece for whatever reason.

So now you are talking with the police and they suggest that you no longer carry money and never wear expensive jewelry. You get angry! How is it that you must change because of this incident? Why must you be punished and made to re-examine your habits and routines? Why are you going through this and how can you benefit from it? You now have two new grey hairs, lots of attention and support and sympathy and no more jewelry; and now you have two new rules to live by – don't carry money, don't wear expensive jewelry. Are you going to buy *into* this new reality or do you choose to create good from this situation?

Here is how you begin to create good. Go back to your walk to work. You are happy and it's a good day. You are whistling as you walk and someone with a gun approaches you and says, "Give me your money and jewelry." You hesitate and think about running but you decide that money and jewelry are just matter and you can easily create and draw more matter. What if this guy were asking for a bottle of shampoo (also just matter)? Would you be so upset? No, I don't think so. How do we defuse money and expensive items so that we can draw them as easily as inexpensive items? We take their power away and leave them be to flow. Do not *hold on* to your money and jewelry if you want lots of them. It flows. Everything must flow and circulate. Let go and let God is still my best advice.

So, our reluctant victim is now observing this situation with a gun to his ribs and he *decides* to enjoy this game (since he has read God's books, he knows that he asked this being to help him learn to go with the flow in order to increase his own abundance).

So, he looks at his assailant as someone who was invited by him for his own good. Now he gives his money and jewelry and goes on to work. He may or may not call the police and since he dislikes everyone getting involved in his private lessons he decides to "let it all go." "What the hell… it's just stuff and to get new stuff I must let go of old stuff."

So, now his boss comes in and wants to know how his morning walk was and he (you) says, "Great! I met someone I used to know long ago and far away. An old friend who agreed to help me grow"… End of story.

*M*ost of you believe that you are not God. You do not trust that God is me, let alone you. You are so afraid to be God that you have closed down your God like powers. You know the future and you know your own past and you even know who you really are. You communicate telepathically and you even see beyond this dimension. You float free of your body and go into other galaxies and you often visit other planes of reality.

The only problem you have is fear and mistrust. You (body) is *afraid* to go off investigating other worlds because it is so wrapped up in this world. You (astral or spirit) are often impatient with body and its fears and so spirit says, "Fine, I don't have time to deal with a frightened child so I'm splitting and going exploring." Now we have you (body) resenting you (spirit) for leaving it alone. Body is on its own in "matter" and does not know how to move freely and flow. Body *needs* spirit to guide it through density. So now we have body resenting spirit and even questioning whether or not it really wants spirit around.

Eventually body decides that it knows best and can do just fine without spirit. So now spirit returns from its adventures and body is not exactly thrilled to see it. "Who needs you," it says. And of course, spirit is offended that body is being so rude and it gets a little miffed and decides to take off again.

Now you can see my problem in getting you back to God. Not only are you split into other body forms, *you*, this you sitting here reading, is split and separating and fighting. Whatever goes on within will be reflected without, or outside of you, so you can *view* your own reflection. If you see hatred in others – guess why? Yes! You hate you. You are so facetted and split that we may never get all parts of you back together again.

We have a great deal yet to learn and I have only just begun to show you your own true identity. You are so clever that you have cut off parts of you and they don't know that you (or part of them) even exist. This is a very complicated (and yet simple) game you play in order to experience matter. You are not here to be aware and enlightened. You purposely shut down so you could hide the fact that you are God. How can you become matter when you know that you are God and *nothing* is impossible? Nothing *is* solid and nothing is transparent. Everything just *is* when you are God.

So; you (God) decided to go within and go unconscious and forget to be God in order to *experience* at a new level. So far the experience has been wonderful and enlightening and delightfully funny to watch. Many watch you, you know? You are very entertaining and now it's time to end your little game and take off your blindfold and come home, because God has a new exciting game for you to learn.

Oh, I see. You don't desire excitement any longer. Well then, I suggest if you're looking for peace and happiness you start letting go of excitement. You are holding it very tight and it runs all through your lives. Excitement is ruling on this plane. All movies contain violence or chance or winning or even losing. All are connected to excitement. A great many jobs are also connected to excitement and travel and glamour, or just simply the excitement of winning whether it's a commission or just a blue ribbon.

It's exciting to watch television too. You get so excited, or sometimes upset, by what you see. You even live your lives around movies and news schedules. Don't give way to excitement if what you really want is peace and calm. Many of you would find a life of peace and calm very boring and mundane at this point in time. You are so *into* excitement that you have produced something exciting for everyone to talk about and participate in… it is called war! And anyone who discusses it or participates is part of this war. If you take part by getting involved in even the smallest way then it is your war. You may have *your* war, it is what you wanted to show you a thrill, and you can blame the other countries or blame your own country's government, but it's really all yours.

Don't get so *involved*. It's not what you really want… not the God you!

*F*or once I do believe we are beginning to "open" to love. You are now beginning to "see" how hatred and violence do not get you what *you* want. That is pretty much what you are here for. You are here to win and get what you want. Why not? Why should it be considered bad to come out on top? It is not. The only problem we have with winning is the excitement and greed and especially control that now rides with it. It is not simply winning any longer. It has taken on a whole new meaning. One must lose for one to win. Why do you think you created that one? It is fear.

You remember in Book Two how I explained Tommy and Suzie and creation – the Gazelle and the Mermaid? Competition came into play, and when you begin to make one cell better than another cell, the main body gets off balance. So how do we bring body back into balance? Right… we make all cells equal. And how *on earth* can we possibly show you how *all are* equal? We take you back to who you really are.

In the same way that characters in a play are equal but only "playing" the king or the queen, you are equal and only playing president and ruler or pauper and thief. You are *not* the *role* that you chose to play. You are simply an actor and not a very good one at that. You got so caught up in your role that you actually began to hate those who were hated in the script. You forgot to simply "act" hurt and began to "feel" pain as if it were real. It is not real. It is only an illusion that became so believed that it *now is part of you.*

So; how does God convince his own body to let go of this pain that it carries? Communication! Yes, communicate with all parts of you (God) and all parts will begin to *know* that we are "one" and "we all go together." So; how does one cell convince the other cells to wake up to the fact that we are one giant body killing parts of itself in an illusionary play? You don't. Leave the other cells to their own dreams and imaginations and creative force. Their path is not your path and your path is definitely not theirs.

So, I see you are confused. After all, if we are all one then what they do affects what I do – right? No, not necessarily. Only through your permission may you receive another's karma or current. Do not request to learn karmically and do not get involved with their stuff – their lessons, their pain. Stop becoming part of everyone else's reality by consent. No one can affect you. No one can give you pain. No one can give you cause to worry. Get your ego out of this. You do not *own* your neighbor so why boss him or her around. You do not own your relatives so why tell them what is right or wrong for them. And, hardest of all for you to swallow, you do not *own* your child – an extremely delicate situation for me to address.

No, you do not own that sweet little babe or even that screeching adolescent. They belong to God. The main body is what contains all cellular development. You are simply guiding and caring for small Gods. Let go of your belief that you are responsible for the actions of these spirits. Quite often when you opened your body to "receive" an invited, or often times uninvited guest, you were learning to overcome your own fears. Well, if your fears are great your child will do as you requested and mirror them for you in a very big way.

Now; most important to remember is that there are no children except that *all* are children. And of course, there are no adults except that *all* are adults. *All cells are exactly identical in reality.* So, how is it that you have this poor defenseless small person holding tightly to you and screaming for love and guidance? This is what *you* requested to learn your own lessons. So, maybe this very open and unusually talented "cell" guided you into position for him/her to enter *through* your body. We of course, all know in this class that it is not necessary to procreate in this fashion. But for now it seems to be the "fad" on earth.

So, now we have this extremely talented spirit who checks into your body and he/she says, "Oh great, I'm going to love being guided and cared for and taught by this spirit, because she has great compassion and sympathy and love." So you say, "Oh hi, I didn't know you were coming, but since you are here I will help you."

Now comes the tricky part for me to explain without upsetting you and getting *you* all riled up and ready to attack. You see, you love to attack when your beliefs are threatened, and since I'm not available to most of you through your own choice, you will be so silly as to attack these books, or even Liane should you find her.

So, let me put this as gently as I can. You may or may not take responsibility for your children. It really does not matter and you are not horrible if you choose to leave them. All agreements are flexible in God's body and all agreements are simply God talking to God, or God interacting with God. No big deal really – if you wish to *carry* another cell (within this body) on your back then that is your choice and it works just fine. If you do not wish to carry the others and you put them down to swim for themselves, this too is fine and works very well. All ways are good. All ways work and all ways are God's ways, because there is nothing but God.

So, don't feel guilty if you no longer wish to be a parent. Parenting is done mostly to "receive" love from a small, inanimate plaything. And when the doting parents soon discover that this tiny form is anything but inanimate, their dreams of a prefect "little love machine" soon disappear in a pile of laundry and late night feedings. It is okay to give up your babies to those who are better prepared to take care of them, and I do not wish you to carry guilt for doing so. Your guilt will put out this light. It is too dense for you to carry. "Love you" – not "love all small children and old people before you." *You are* all and all are you. Do not put you last. You are not less than, and it is a sin to treat yourself as such. Sin of course, is simply a way of saying "without love." Don't be without love of self. Do not sin against God (you)!

❧

*V*ery often you do not wish to hear what is. So, very often I must sneak up on you with certain information.

The information in God's books is given in such a way as to open your subconscious and sneak past your conscious or ego self. If you find information unacceptable it is your own *fear* of this truth. If you find you have no problem with such information, it may be that you have already "realized" this truth, or that part of you who has objections may be buried very deep within you and unable to express their views at this time. So, there is no way that one cell is ahead of or more advanced than the other cells. A mass murderer may be uncovering hidden beliefs and emotions that are solidly impacted or frozen into another's subconscious, and they appear to be pleasant and loving only because they have not yet come to that layer.

Remember my story in Book Five about the giant onion and how you are peeling off *your* layers to come home with only spirit? Well, this is how you do this. Most of you are un-layering and learning a great deal about your own self and how you view life. Others are sitting in front of their television watching football and soap operas and they worry only about how the characters and players will win! This is not boredom for them. This is excitement and living. How do you know that they have not already peeled their onion far beyond your layers and have learned most of what you are now learning? Maybe they have already gone back to God and returned to this life just to show you how to live. If you see someone who does not get concerned with what goes on around them and who never gets upset by much in the way of news, watch them closely.

Now; I know that I have confused you again. How do you expect me to teach you if you do not allow me to show you both sides of God? God does not fit into one neat little category. You have always given God his place by comparing his energy by your energy. You give God what is his identity by casting *your* image upon him – your attitudes and beliefs of what God is or should be. *I am not made in your image and likeness no matter what you may think. God is his own creator and I do not create according to your rules.* You are so multifaceted that you can't even begin to view yourself, let alone view God in his entirety.

God is not your image of him so stop pushing *your* image on my children. God is God and you are God, so how do you expect to tell another who is God how to act or behave? God does not wish you to judge those who you view as slow or stupid or unenlightened. You don't even know who you are so how can you judge others as not good enough to be God? Those who sit and watch T.V. and drink beer and eat candy and grow fat may just be you – a parallel you who began to *live* in order to help teach this you something about life.

So; stop judgment against *any* because *all* are

actually you. Not only are all you, but all were created by you! Now you see how far we have to go in our learning process, so I hope you will stop putting yourself in the position of teacher and know-it-all. Give it a rest. After all, you don't even know how *you* got here, that shows how bright you are. As Liane tells her friends, "We must all be dumb as a box of rocks. We have a brain and we shut down ninety-five percent of it. Then we started poisoning ourselves with chemicals. No wonder aliens come here and do experiments on us. They can't figure out how we could be so haywire.

Imagine watching some small species of animal, who kill one another for no reason and often times commit suicide in droves and even eat poison. Not to mention all the other crazy habits we have, like loving to watch murder and destruction of property (movies and T.V.). So, if you were a scientist or had an advanced mind or even just curiosity, wouldn't you want to help these silly animals and find out what the malfunction is? Maybe that's what all this business about aliens abducting people and probing is all about. Maybe they think they're doing good, like we often do when we explore other life forms for 'research.' Anyway, it's just a thought."

So, this is how Liane sees our position in this dimension at this time. It does make you wonder doesn't it? And how does God fit into a body that is "dumb as a box of rocks?" It's difficult – very, very difficult. But God is breaking through and his children are learning acceptance and humility.

Humility is a "biggie," for you have thought yourself so clever for so long and now to admit, "No, I don't have the answers. As a matter of fact I don't even know who or what I am" is a very good place to be. Most of you become so sure of yourselves because you must have a point of reference, a view point so to speak. Because without this point of reference you feel ungrounded and insecure. I want you to be ungrounded and insecure. As I have told Liane, she cannot hold God if her arms are busy holding on to security. You must be "free flowing" and unattached to any belief and any matter. *Let go and let God move you.*

Now, for those of you who are too *afraid* to let go of your present belief, I suggest you stay right where you are until you are ready. No one moves another without mutual consent, so I hope you each allow one another your own beliefs as there is no wrong belief and no wrong way back to God.

After all, you never left God… remember? See – you don't know who you are so top telling others who they are. This will do for now as Liane is going to take me out today!

ҳ℮ℹℓ℮ℳ

Once I get you to "see" how you are all one, you will stop judgment. Judgment allows you to separate and identify with those you "believe" to be *like*. How can you not be *like* someone when you are that someone? Stop saying that part of God is bad or wrong. Who gave you the choice to set yourself up as judge and jury? – Oh yes, I guess I did, didn't I? I am you and I gave you permission to do whatever it takes to become God in matter.

I guess I have a big job to do in convincing God (me… you) that I am now taking some weight off you by allowing you to give your choices over to God. You do not know who you are, and you do not know how to be God.so I am inviting you to ask me into your lives. Now would be a good time to go back and reread our first three books; *God Spoke through Me to Tell You to Speak to Him, No One Will Listen to God* and *You Are God*. These three simple text books allow you to let go of your fear of evil and God.

You each carry fear that prevents you from seeing how you are God, and when you let go of fear you will be God – in awareness of your true identity for the first time since entering matter. You will not be left behind no matter how "thick" you may think you are. You are God and *all* parts of God do indeed wake up. No one is left behind no matter how awful they may appear in your world.

Most of you believe that to be good you must follow rules. What if you moved to a new dimension with all new rules? You may not like your new rules at first but you would adjust and become comfortable with them after a time. In the same way that your teenage son can be taken into military service and taught that it is okay to kill under certain conditions, you too can be taught to break your own rules.

So far the biggest problem with *your* rules is that you don't apply them to you alone. You are so busy forcing others to comply with *your* rules that it's a wonder you have any energy left to love. Oh, maybe that's the problem. Maybe we spend so much time devoting our lives to doing everything "right," that we don't have time to just simply love one another and accept one another as unique and yet the same. Maybe the guilt that compounds each time we break the rules we enforce on ourselves, as well as our children and our spouses and even our neighbors, is so powerful that it takes all of our energy just to survive our own mistakes and judgments. Maybe, if God could get you each to just stop preaching the horrors of this world long enough – I could get you to see how you are wasting your own life force energy and giving your power away to fear.

Stop throwing you away on ridiculous ideas of control and fear. Begin to *allow* all to experience in their own way. Stop living out of fear of what may or may not take place if you surrender your control. Give up power because you are using it in such a way that you are creating a belief in pain, and pain does not really exist. Don't you see? If I can just get you to "look" at all differently, you may begin to see without pain and you may even begin to understand how you have turned everything upside down and even backward, just to confuse you so you would not wake up to the fact that you are all there is. There is no other power. There is no evil and there is no danger.

Let go – give up to God what is God's. Don't fight to be right! Just say, "I don't know and let everyone else believe whatever they wish and don't be concerned with anything. That is true power. The power of love and acceptance to the point of handing it all over to the part of you that remembers God and how you got here.

Yes, part of you knows, but that part has been

shut down and turned off and buried under mounds of past programming and density. It's time to come "alive" my children, this is the greatest of times. The game is over. The "jig" is up! Stop pretending because it's time to become real. This is not your true reality. This is simply a game you chose to play to stop you from seeing "all" that you are. You have played many tricks on yourself and you have disguised you in order to investigate your own existence. It is *all* God, in *all* forms, creating as God, to confuse God, so that the extent of God's vastness might be known.

God began to contemplate and imagine how it might be and all the various way's it might be, and each thought took on a life of it's own and stretched out, or actually inward, to create more dimensions and layers and steps to the ladder. We could go on and on and on and… well, you get the idea. But it's best to regroup our thoughts and draw "in" the information that has been gained and the energy that is stuck in other areas. All parts of God must now return to God in order for order to reign and chaos to end. Enough of pain and fear and ego gain. We are now moving on to peace and love and Godliness. Won't you join us on this new adventure in God's expansion and growth? You are all invited and even all parts of each of you.

So, God is going to return to himself in order to

show himself all that he has become, and you are God, so I guess you must be ready to come home. You *are* invited you know? Don't be afraid my child. Let go of your old way of viewing life and even death. Begin to know that you are God by putting your trust in God and allowing him free reign over your life. It's not all bad and it's not all fun and games. Taking away old beliefs is often painful only because you choose to believe in pain. God is into painless love, not love that hurts. To change your ways is often very difficult but it's really the only reason you are here. It is not possible to "become" without change, and God is always in a constant state of becoming.

So; continue to become God as God comes to greet you. These are marvelous times and God is now on the rise and being born "into" matter. God is no longer locked behind bars up in the clouds. No more stories of judgment day and pearly gates. There are no bars keeping me from you. I am no longer a prisoner of your thoughts. I am free and writing and living and breathing in matter. Not that I have not before now, but you would not allow it before now. Now it is known and accepted.

God is accepted on earth therefore God exists on earth. Without invitation and acceptance it was just a dream. Now it is reality – your reality because *you* chose to believe it. What you believe is what you get. And to believe that God only exists in heaven with angels keeps God in heaven with angels. I am now free to enter matter as I have now come to earth through the free will of a few. Please invite me to take over your life and show you life without pain and confusion. It may take a little time, but the emotional and physical rewards will be so worthwhile.

I must go now as I have totally zapped my pen. She thinks she's going to fall apart, but she won't. She just needs some attention. Good day to each and every one of you.

⁂

So far we have not upset any of you with news you do *not* wish to hear. Most of you have been ready and even *prepared* for this information. You may feel that it is a complete surprise and even coincidence that you purchased or came across this series. It is not an accident nor is it coincidence. It is a planned chain of events in your life. Most of you expect to be taken "up" when you leave this plane. You don't even know how, or why, or even that you "expect" this incident to occur.

Loving Light, Book 7

You do, however, know that you are going somewhere.

Most of you believe that you are going to grow old and die and go "out there" somewhere. You do not realize that this belief *creates* this reality. So, how do I get you to stop dying and stay here to *transform* body? I lock you into a new belief pattern and you begin to break away from mass consciousness and pack thinking, and you actually start to agree with this idea of transformation. This "idea" is based *in* a reality that has a much "lighter" vibration than your dense three dimensional thinking.

Most often your thoughts are so dense that they literally connect directly to dense vibratory modes that are already in place around your hemisphere. Most of these patterns are set *in place* similar to a webbing system. In the same way that you are wired into your beliefs and programming, this entire dimension is wired into a particular pattern. We now have layer over layer of cross webbing, and the ultimate course of action is to eliminate the web system. This of course, takes some work since we do not wish to frighten you humans further.

So; all parts of you are now beginning to work with God to *release* you (this you) from the web of lies and inconsistencies that you have chosen to hide behind. And what is the *biggest* lie of all? You bet... it's a belief that God is not you and that God is someone outside of yourself. So, as we begin to untangle these webs of untruth and falsehood we begin to *expose* you to reality. It is often painful because of past programming in this dimension as to what reality is. So, for the most part, the utmost in care is being taken. I tell you repeatedly not to push your loved ones and even your neighbor to "wake up," because waking up to you is painful because you choose to carry painful thoughts and ideas.

I have a story to tell you. This is actually Liane's story but she does not wish me to write about her, so I will tell you this story. It starts with the "idea" that in the islands of the South Pacific it was once the custom to intermarry. Husbands and wives were often brother and sister; and oh how they loved one another. Can you imagine your mother and father saying how happy you will be some day because you will marry your family loved one and create beautiful babies and even rule as king and queen? And so it was. King and queen were often related and sometimes as *close* as a brother or sister.

Now we have a time of great change in our islands and the fine folks of religion come to *share* their teachings with the unenlightened natives. Can you imagine the horror of these fine "God fearing" people when they discover that the natives of Hawaii actually intermarry and have sex with one another?

So, these God fearing people begin to "teach" our loving natives to adore God and to give homage to "one" God not several Gods, and to not sleep with your relatives. So what happened to the little boy and girl who were now told that everything their parents said was wrong? It is now a sin in God's eyes for brother to love sister sexually. We must now create an entire new belief system for these poor misinformed natives. And who should create this new belief system? Well, the God fearing ones, of course. Do not get me wrong here. There are no victims, remember?

So now these missionaries are busy changing the ways of this little island and addressing the problem of nudity and outrageous dancing and even promiscuity. And it takes these new found teachers quite some time to convince these poor under-educated natives to don such long dresses with such high necklines and sleeves. It was even silly to argue with the teachers because it quickly became known throughout the island that education and contemporary ideas were now here, and those who did not follow suit were outcasts and not accepted by the new rulers. You see, this little island lost it's monarchy to society and its rules. Weak fearful people draw weak fearful teachers. So – no victims here.

Now, to get to Liane's portion of this story… Liane wonders what we would all be like if we were raised on an island in the middle of this universe, and our teachers were our parents, and of course we all know that mom and dad don't teach what's bad. They only teach good. So, we're all born on this island and into our chosen family, and when we begin to grow our parents begin to teach us about life and love and caring and sharing. Mom and dad start by teaching how we are all from God and how God loves us and *never* judges us ever!

So now we get to the stuff about growing up and sharing sex; and our parents explain how sex is fun and good as all activities on our island. And when you are ready for sex you may choose *any* consenting partner. It's not necessary to hide sex — because it's a "good thing." It is a way of showing affection and it is a way of having a very good time. When the question of partners comes up, your parents explain that anyone can be a partner in sex just as anyone can be a partner in a game or at a dance. So now we have mom and dad teaching us to love through sex and not be ashamed of this simple, pleasant act. And of course if we choose, we may make love with, or have sex with our brother or sister or father or mother, and of course there will be no trauma because it is not made into a big horror show.

So, how would that be… can you imagine? No pain and no trauma attached to sex. No more than dancing. I am here to teach you to let go of this hold you have on judgment. Judgment creates pain and pain causes guilt and guilt is such a heavy burden to carry that you finally die from carrying it. Drop dead if you must but please don't teach my children to be *God fearing*. I love you and I love them, and love does not co-exist with fear. So; who are you – love, or fear and judgment?

Let's stop all this silliness. There is much bigger work to do than frightening yourselves and others by your belief in right and wrong, or good and bad. Let it all go my children, let the cobwebs fall away and begin to see from spirit and love. It will do you no good to *hold* to your present belief in evil, because it does not exist. There is only me here. I am God and I will continue to teach you until you begin to believe the truth. Let go of this burden you carry. Put down judgment. Its weight is killing you and I want you to live!

❧

So long ago I began to investigate all concepts of myself. To my own delusion I began to order new parts based on old rules. I have not been God for more than a blink of an eye and I often do not agree with who I am. I am God. I am Satan, I am love. I am hate. I am guilt, I am judgment. I am outrageous behavior and I am sentiment. Most often however, I am becoming and growing and learning and dissolving and re-integrating my own beingness.

I do not choose to be. I simply am. I do not *accept* my beingness, it simply is. I do not judge what I am or how I got where I am. I simply am. I am not as you believe me to be and for the most part I am a great deal *more* than I actually know. *I was once, am now and always will be.* Not too exciting am I? Just God being... not struggling to be, but being. Not searching to know, but knowing. *You* are the part that struggles and searches and strives for excellence. I am God and you are God. You said, "I will go into matter to see how it 'feels' to *be* in matter." I said, "fine, I will stay here and watch and wait and see how well you do."

You went, I stayed. You are my other half or my inner self. You are me having this "idea" in material form. You are all me moving around in me, only by consent from me, only because *you* gave consent before you went within to see how it would be to be within the whole of God. Now you are so deep "within" or "in trance" that you believe you are alone and that I am outside of you. I am not outside of anything. I never left, I never changed, I always am just being.

So now you are afraid of God because the fear of Jesus or God has been programmed into your memory cells. And all the while that you fear God you are actually fearing you. So; how do I bypass all of your programming so that half of God is not fearing the other half of God? I take "one" cell and clean it and reprogram it to suit my needs to contact my other half and I clean out this cell physically, emotionally and vibrationally; and I begin to transmit signals and letters and books of information to the other cells who still are dormant and in trance from mounds of programming. Next I integrate this cell back into position to have an effect on other cells who are swaying to this certain vibrational pattern.

It's all very simple actually. God acted as a mechanic and ignited a cell in order to have that ignited cell kick start or jump start others. One is all it takes and one is all there really is. Of course you won't "see" this clearly for some time.

So, what are the effects on the initial cell? Well, she's had a rough time understanding how she could be involved and even how this all occurred. Mostly she does not believe that it (this entire episode in her life) is "real." But then what is real and who is real... you or me? You call me Spirit, I call you Idea. So who's more real?

Anyway, this original ignited cell has been hurt by her own belief in pain and by her belief in being "accepted and acceptable." Mostly she feels let down that God has not delivered her from pain and confusion and even self-pity. And what she doesn't understand is that God is doing just that. God has reversed her spin in order to spin her back out of this three dimensional dream. As she reversed spin she began to lose parts of her self; her life as she knew it, her identity and her toys. So this is how God gets you creating from light vibration. I must reverse spin to re-collect you. To retrieve what is God it is necessary to pull the strings back in on the yo-yo (you). You have been spinning *out* from God and now you are spinning back home.

Now; in the beginning you did not travel. You simply were, just as I am. Now you begin to get a little movement and this movement created a charge, sort of like electricity. And oh, how good this was to see and feel. You have tried to re-create this charge by moving you into other positions "within" God. Now we have you doing your own thing, only without you there is no God. You are independent in action yet connected to the rest of God. Sort of like a heart that does its thing "within" the body and yet it is not the "whole" you.

So; now we have this you getting a thrill out of this charge of electric current, or energy, that you create by movement. And how did you learn to move? You simply moved your idea into a new position. So now we have idea taking on a whole new dimension and idea begins to move and move and create more and more charge, and soon "all" parts begin to *feel* this charge and get stimulated to the point of movement. Now we have all these parts "inside" God and they are splitting and shaking and jumping and popping and carrying on like a giant fire works display. Oh yes, you remember how it was and you now duplicate as much as possible.

So, you're now jumping and quaking and moving and grooving on electric charge. Some call this the Big Bang Theory. It's actually very accurate compared to many of *your* theories. Anyway, this charge builds and explodes and multiplies and is becoming something very, very encompassing. Now we have a short-out or blown fuse. Parts of this body of ether or Godness are so burnt to the extent that they settle back into position with a dull thud. They are now dark and charred and no longer vibrating. They blew their own self out by creating friction, and they settled into a position of *non-movement* because they no longer wanted to fry to death from their own friction. Friction heats you up until you fry from the sparks that you create and yet you enjoy friction because it is movement against the self. *All friction is simply rubbing against.*

This is how wars begin. No one on this planet is yet ready for peace. Peace would be too cumbersome and restraining for you. We must reverse the initial spin that created the first charge of friction. When you have eliminated the first spin, simply by reversing it, you will be on your way into a new direction as if you never spun "out" in the first place. It's like going down a road that has a dead end or *death* at the end, and instead of going all the way you simply turn around, go back, and take the other road that has a freeway all the way to forever-ever land. This is good for now.

$\mathcal{S}$o far we have been unable to *show* love to this dimension. Mostly it is hidden behind desire, revenge, loneliness and wanting. Love is basically acceptance and allowing. When you accept without condition, you love. You have not had much experience with this type of love and often spend an entire lifetime "working" at changing your mate or loved one.

Most often you do not realize that what you feel is not love. Most of you are drawn through the electrical "charge" emitted by this charge. Most electrical current runs through you as well as around you and when a charge is in place it emits more of itself. Most charges have been created through friction. Friction causes a charge to send out and immerse into whatever matter is involved.

Most of what you *carry* in this life is charge. This charge is no longer available for energy since it is now *stuck* in you or your neighbor. If you have a giant fight it causes friction and charge results. This charge is in matter or form, which is you. You carry this charge with you through your memory banks and it appears lifetime after lifetime. So; when you begin to approach someone for the first time you may have a strong feeling toward this person. They may not be the one who engaged you so generously in battle when you had your big fight, however, they may carry that same charge from their own battles. Now you meet this new person and instantly you like them. They "feel" familiar somehow and you want to know them better. This is mutual charge or like attracts like.

So now we have you falling in love with this person because for you, at this time, love means having common qualities so you won't have to disagree all the time. So now we have you married to this person and you find areas that are not so common and you want to change these little annoyances about your partner. So, how do we *change* what we don't like in someone else? Right – we don't. We change how we are viewing this entire situation. And soon enough your loved one will begin to change to suit you because he or she loves the way you "adapt" to them. This is mostly on a personal level and when it comes to larger situations numbering in the hundreds or thousands or millions of souls involved, it is simply a matter of one "letting go and letting God" and all else will fall into place as planned.

If it's not your business, stay out of it. If it is your business, get out of it by not hanging on to it. Either way you are being a non-participant and allowing charge to settle elsewhere. This is why Christ taught to turn your other cheek. There is no pain without resistance. Allow all to flow and all will flow. This is especially important while you are "learning" to be God again. The more involved you become, the more friction. The less involved – the less friction. The less friction – the less charge or pain. The less charge – the more "energy" or "life force" or "God force" reigns.

☙❧

*O*ften it is thought that you do not "belong" to God. How could you when you are so dangerous to your own self as well as to those who oppose you?

You begin your life on earth as an infant. You then grow and learn or take on information. This information and teaching becomes who you are. You "decide" at each turn whether or not you will accept certain truths as your own. In this way you begin to create your own world. You each *live* inside what might be called an energy field of thoughts and dreams and ideas. You *are* energy and you create energy as you burst or expand. The movement, or friction, or expansion, is what pushes you outward into new areas of your own self-discovery.

So, how can you possibly know who you are if you are not yet complete? You *are* complete and yet you are growing in size, only you cannot grow in size because you take up all time and space as God. So what exactly *is* occurring and how do you become God, or more of who and what you really are? You begin by being you. Stop pretending to be what you believe to be acceptable. You must become who and what you are and who and what you are is God. So; first off stop pleasing them because they are just as unconscious as the rest. Start with you and know that you are now moving forward in a direct path to God. There actually is no movement taking place, but since you depend on time/space association to show progress we will use these terms.

Most of you are spinning atoms and you have no concept of your own whereabouts. Most of you spin and weave a pattern that is contributing to the webbing network that forms camouflage for the disguising of God. So now we must remove this webbing system that has been so astutely put in place.

Most all have contributed to this game but now the game is no longer necessary. We are moving on to a new awareness, and to continue to dig yourselves into this hole of deception is no longer how you will improve yourselves. You must now move to the point of "acceptance" in order to receive full return to your natural state. Acceptance begins with knowledge that judgment "holds on" to, and soon leads to the awareness that to flow is to move freely and to unclog or disperse trapped energy. Energy must be freely moved and received and accepted in order for it to return. Do not hold on to old ideas and beliefs. You are not in danger and no one is dangerous or threatening. No one is going to harm you, as it is impossible to have harm. Harm does not exist. Only pain is and this is only an illusion created by false interpretation.

Most of you do not know how to "accept" and so you blame and cause your own kind of harm. This is done on many levels and within many dimensions. Most harm is caused *through* judgment and most judgment is drawn from one not accepting "all" as good and right and wonderful and part of God. How can you begin to point and say, "how awful" when you do not know what you are viewing?

It is quite unusual to see others as though you were their own self, or even to see your own self as a reflection created by another. Well, hold on to your hats because you are just a reflection and nothing more. You are "idea" without purpose. You are a great reflective shield that stops and reverses what "is" into its exact opposite. *You* have turned God around and in on himself, in order to view himself, or you (your own self).

You are so misinformed as to who you are and what your place is that you are playing both sides of this game, or mirror, and you do not even know that it is you. And the one you judge is, more than likely, more you than this you who is being reflected out. Don't get too excited about what you see or "think you see" in this world. You are viewing a reflection that is reversed and distorted just to show God all angles and areas of the unknown. How do you reverse God? You show him himself from within and make it *look* like it is out, but it is not. It is simply *idea* taking shape and form, and you place so much emphasis on idea that you are stuck in it. It is not real! Get out! Wake up! Shift gears… move ahead.

Stop pretending to "be" when you are the sender not the receiver. You are God not human. You never came to "be." I had an "idea," a thought, a moment of concentration, and in the moment you were born… only you were not. You were simply and are simply a thought that manifested into matter when in actuality the thought was never meant to "be." It was only meant to idealize itself not to materialize in form that cannot move.

So; lighten up! Accept everything as good and God, and move on to idea in light, not form. God is reversing and coming out. He is waking up from his thought or daydream, and "idea" is now being rolled back within itself to form more God awareness.

So far you have not become "aware" that you are not here at all. And, of course, with all this confusion concerning good and evil we have a great deal of judgment pinning us down. Think how it would be to allow "everyone" to do exactly as they pleased. Yes, everyone! So some guy decides to shoot you. So what?

Let him. What if you *knew* that *you* do not die… ever? Now this thought becomes no more difficult than some guy pointing his finger and saying, "Bang! You're dead." You say, "Okay, fine" and go on about your day. That's how it *really* is you know? No death, no disease and no danger. It does not really exist.

❧

Now I will begin my definition of love. This is at the request of Janet, a very dear friend to my pen.

So far most are concerned with giving and caring and feeling equal in time and space. You do not choose who you love but you do choose how you love.

You do not regard "all" to be "acceptable" and from where you stand in your storm of misinformation this is quite explainable. Certain types simply do not meet your standards or requirements and therefore you refuse to "engage" yourself emotionally with those who are of this category. So far you are not only choosy; you are even selective in your friends and acquaintances. You have developed your own skills and attitudes and you do not wish to "step down," so to speak, to the level of an undesirable. This, of course, has created *friction* all through your history. Not that friction is bad... nothing is *bad*. Friction is just not what you are after at this time. I suggest "peace." It is most conducive to the spirit that is God.

Now; in this selectiveness, you began to create greater separation and division of God – or good and bad were born. We now have the good guys and the bad guys. Most of the good guys are made up of those who follow rules. They do what is "right," they act harmoniously, they live a "clean" life; they even say their prayers (most often). So the opposite of good is now reflected as bad. This roster is made up of those who break the rules. Those who don't cover their true "feelings" regarding certain situations that are deemed "proper," and they often spoke their own mind and offended many who knew that the rule was to follow decorum or what is proper.

Sometimes to be bad was considered "in" and "cool" and even "current," or fashionable. We seem to have repeated this cycle often during your history pattern.

Now; most of you at this time are so confused because you have played good guy and you have played bad guy, each so often that you have programming relating to each position. You have so much friction built from "bad guy" times that you often judge your own self as bad when you do not agree with current choices. This friction also affects the programming known as "good guy." It is so tossed and torn as to *what is* or is not okay that it creates guilt at every turn.

Now; when you fall "in" love, you simply expand a version of your own "idea" of good-guy-self and send this expanded reflection into your energy field. Most often this good guy version that you "order" carries both negative and positive factors from your own field of energy. You may believe that you "draw" to you, but in actuality you receive your own image in the form of another you, standing in front of you and saying exactly what you *really* believe in your own dual, vast selves.

This is how you draw "all" to you. So this is why I say to look into your mirror and do not "fix" them – fix you. You will wish to know that you are also sending partners or reflections from other unconscious parts of this self. If you have parts of you who hate you because they have believed themselves to be "abused" by this you, they will surely send you a reflection that is not too often pleasant. Don't "hate" any, as "any" is all you and you will be creating more hatred of the self by unknown parts of self.

So; when you "accept" all parts by allowing them to be you, you will be loving you… all of you. And in accepting these parts, by accepting the fact that they are your own reflection and not some monstrous "bad" guy who is hassling you, you will be "receiving" them as part of you. Some parts of you have never been acknowledged by you and therefore cannot stand you and will do whatever they can to disturb you; just as a small child who is born to negligent parents will (when grown) do whatever it takes (even rob a bank or shoot someone) to get some attention or simply acknowledgment that they "belong" to you.

Do not ignore who you send. Do show them kindness and courtesy. It is not necessary to move strangers into your home unless, or course, you feel that strongly towards your own reflection. It is kind enough to be gentle and firm if one of your reflections pursues you or insists on causing problems. Let them know that you too have your own pain but do allow them the courtesy of "acknowledgment."

It is not often that "one" of you will approach you and insist on attention in a direct fashion, it is however very common for strangers to get you a little riled up, or as you say, "push your buttons." When this occurs, "look" at your reflection and know that you sent them because you are beginning to put God back together. If you push back at a reflection it will simply find another way to show you who *you are*.

Most often these reflections show love and kindness and caring. You often push even these away. You are so tired of boring people and to "accept" more boring people into your life begins to bore you. So you are being bored by you out of a need for excitement. Often you will "feel" the need to be excited and have more fun so you draw or produce a little "friction" to stir things up and get you going. Then you settle back down to "cool your jets," and calm and peace feel very good. Soon you will learn how to make peace without excitement and how to have love not war.

⚜

*O*kay! We have established so far that you are not God. Oh, you believe you are, but you're really just "thought" in form. For once I want to convince you of this, so I will tell you a story.

You believe yourselves to be so nothing and so unimportant. What if I were to explain how you really are? What if I could find the exact letters to make up the true language that would put this picture of existence into your conscious mind? I think you might fall down on your knees and thank God that you don't really belong behind the mask that you chose to wear.

Okay, so far we have you "seeing" how you might be God because you came from this huge expanded consciousness that calls itself God, but do you really feel like God? And if you feel like a God, what (on earth) does that mean? And if you feel like a failure at this God business, does that automatically leave you "out" of God, or do you become God by believing you are human and living for God? Well, I will explain. My story is brief as my pen is in no condition to write for me right now.

Once upon a time, I began to blow-off-steam. Steam is what occurs when heat and friction begin to cool and slow and densify. So, God is cooling off after a great "show" of expression in various colors and shapes and I now want to "particle" myself in order to feel "individual" or separate. I, of course, am not separate. However, if I choose to concentrate only on my big toe, does that mean that my head goes numb or my legs or my navel? Or do all parts continue to function and lock and unlock barriers and blocks into other areas of self?

And once I put my attention, or focus, on this big toe do I lose contact with other parts of my body or do I continue to push parts of God into all parts of self to keep self alive? And if I put my consciousness into every-living-and-non-living being and stone, how do they know that they have consciousness of their own? Or does all consciousness begin in God and flow outward or is there an "in" place in God for anything to come forth from? And if God created all that is, how is it that he got it all so messed up – or is it messed up? What if God just *thought* "Gee, I think I'll try this," or "Gosh, maybe that will be best," and along come these thoughts in form and begin to bombard the sender only no one "sent" anything. Form can take off in the blink of an (earth) eye and you are simply a thought that is in form for just a mere blink!

Lighten up… go home to God or stay put; it doesn't really "matter" because there isn't any matter. You are not…

∾⧂∽

So far, most of you have decided that it is not so important to be God and "rise" as it is to maintain comfort in this 3rd dimensional world. Most often you are faced with your own responsibilities and pressures and family and job. So, I will continue to write through Liane until more of you are *available* to me for my use. I have begun to *gain* a foothold within matter and this is good. Now, you will wish to know that I do not recognize *your* responsibilities and commitments as anything important, as *nothing* really is important to each individual and, of course, this is relative to how your guilt and responsibility push you.

So far most of you are afraid to move too quickly toward a new awareness. Oh, I know, you read and ask questions and even search for your answers, and of course a better way. The tough part here is to get you to *accept* the better way without too much pain and confusion on your part. You can't see from where *you* are how it could be better to have *no* responsibilities to hold you back. You want responsibilities so you may become a "responsible" person. And who taught you that? Everyone who never wanted to take responsibility for their own self... and most of you don't. You can't even get your body and your spirit to live in perfect harmony, so you project your attention elsewhere and convince others to do so also. So now we have everyone getting all riled up and excited over poverty and starvation and war, and I will tell you now that this is simply a way of ignoring the work that is waiting for you right inside of you.

So, how do we get you to stop fixing them and begin to fix you? Simple. Do enema. It's cheap, it's easy and it works. How can this help you clean up your own mess? Simple. You are garbage from all you eat and you are energy (blocked) from all you think. Enema releases garbage and drains the blocked energy. What goes in must come out… circulation is life. Stop circulation; you then stop life. Continue to circulate, and continue to grow in life as well as expansion. You now "shrink" with old age because you are no longer taking on energy or giving out energy. Circulation slows down and stops. With enema, the channels of circulation begin to change and grow and expand as more room in you is created for "life" to enter.

You begin to expand instead of shrink and shrivel. This, of course, does not occur over night but will be a gradual process. It is similar to cleaning out any garbage system. When a system is plugged you must stop shoveling garbage into it, then clean out what is blocking the system, then get it "flowing" properly again. Enema will clean out the blocked system and strengthen the organs to continue functioning at an exceptional level of ability. And when you stop shoveling in the garbage and begin to feed this system only "live" or natural fuel, you will be well on your way to "expanded" life.

So far it is best to allow you your own time to discover who and what you are. Most of you are so afraid of God that you do not wish to know how you are God. Therefore I will speak of power.

You are not only the power of this universe; you created *all* that you see. You projected thought out into soft virgin air and this air became solid with your command or willful power. Most often you have no "idea" how you create or even when.

In actuality it is difficult to get you to *admit* that you are the creator. You want *your* creator to be big and bold and powerful and able to stand tall when you point your finger and yell, "God, why did you forsake me. Why did you *let* this or that occur." And then you stand back and let it be, only because you convince you that it was God's will. Famine, flood, disease, death; it's all God's will, so you push God further away so he won't *inflict* his will upon you again. The real reason you do not communicate directly with God is out of judgment held against him. Most of you would call him a son of a bitch if you were not so *afraid* of God. God would surely throw you in hell for that one.

So, you can see how we have a great deal of work to do. You must love God enough to express freely to God how you feel toward him. You must not be so afraid of what you are. You are God and you want to kick God for most of what has occurred in your life out of fate or judgment. If God can be treated just as you are treated, you will begin to see how I am you. I won't erupt in an explosion of violence and thunder, so go ahead and dump this anger that you carry.

It is not healthy to *fear* God. Love is the absence of fear and when you love me, you will love a very big part of you; the part of you who creates for you. You are afraid to contact your own creator and explain how you feel. Do it for love. Call God a liar, a hypocrite, a thief, a murderer; whatever you are feeling. None of these are offensive to God. He does murder, he does steal; he does cheat. God is all parts of everything, and everything is God. He won't abuse you for getting your feelings out.

This is your homework for today. Sit down and get good and angry with God. He is waiting to let you let go of your anger. Be gentle with you by expressing *fully* how you really feel. When you heal you of your wound, you will be healing God.

*W*e are not far from being God. We are so "connected" to matter and density that it is very difficult to move "away" from this three dimensional world. You are hooked-in so to speak. Most often you do for the sake of material good or material wealth or matter. You will belong to organizations and hang out with influential members of your community just to be "in" with wealth or power. Often you spend energy convincing others you are "deserving of," when you really have nothing in common with those you wish to impress. You are in your wrong place and you know it. You do not feel happy and you do not feel love for those you deal with; and often you do not feel love for the work you force yourself to do for this material wealth.

Most often, you are so embedded in poverty or planning your future or trying to escape your past that this you suffers greatly and enjoys little. You must begin to be *you*; not them and certainly not who *they* want you to be. *They* do not push you without your approval. Your approval usually stems from disapproval of who you really are.

No one wants to be worthless or useless or unacceptable, so everyone plays this game to get to the top or just simply to survive. You are so afraid to be you that you do not confide your deepest feelings and thoughts out of fear of not being good enough, or just being stupid or dumb enough to be left out when the guys upstairs "choose" Mr. or Miss or Mrs. Right. You are who you are, but you are changing you to fit in. And what I want you to do is be who you are. You are God and you each have a specific role to play. So, if you each change to suit the ideal of another, you lose you. Then I must come along and find you.

You often hear how someone was lost, and prayed and found God. God isn't lost. You are lost. You are lost and afraid and you believe you are in danger. You are not alone. You are hiding out and carrying on like there is no salvation. You have hidden you *in* you. God is inside and outside and all around. You can't lose God. You can however lose "sight" of God.

So, in this book I will teach you how to see God once again. You may touch me and love me as Liane has, she "knows" my hugs and she knows my voice and you too will see and remember. I have not been gone you know? I never left. You just got so frightened that you couldn't hear me through your own screaming and fit throwing. You have screamed and begged and cried, and you never take your hands away from in front of your eyes long enough to *look* at who you are. You are like a child who holds both hands over his eyes when the most awful part of the movie rolls by. You are such a frightened child that many of you cannot accept the fact that God would and does communicate in this world. "Keep God away." That is your motto on earth. "Pray to God and beg his forgiveness but don't dare suggest that he might talk back." Well, I do talk back and I am happy to be *allowed* to do so.

For those of you who try and try to *receive* my words, either written or verbal, I wish you to know that I will keep trying. So please don't give up on me. I must transmit through layers and layers of fear and density. My signal may be weak and you may not *trust* that it is me, but with the "will" in its correct function all will come to pass. You too will begin your path home and you too will carry on conversations with God. And who is God? He is you, of course.

❧

Now that you are beginning to "see" how you are God you are quite concerned. First of course, is the safety factor – "How can I be God and be *responsible* for everything in this world and even this universe?" And – "How can I have God to pray to for help if *I am* God?" And – "How can I ever forgive myself for all that I have blamed on me (God)?"

We have a great deal of work to do in *uncovering* your true identity and it will take some time. But the good news is that you are "open" to hearing your own identity. Most often, getting someone to admit to who and what they are, is the first step to recovering. So, you are each recovering and learning to be a better you, or actually, the only you. You have been hiding the fact that you are God for so long that it will take time to assess how far underground in your subversiveness you went. We will dig you out of your fear and command you to stand tall and face you. You are God and you are hiding from God. So now you must find a way to come to terms with who and what you are.

These books are meant to relieve pain, and in order to relieve pain you must first "see" that you are *in* pain. I believe that this is known as intervention when it is done for someone who is *denying* his alcoholism. This is much the same, as you are denying your Godism. You will be "told" exactly who and what you have done, but you will not be punished as you have suffered greatly already.

This business about dying for your sins has gone

far enough. Jesus did not teach that you must die for your sins or even be punished for them. Jesus taught that there is no death, by rising from what you call death. Jesus taught that no one is punished for your sins, especially you. How did he teach this? He said "Here, give them to me, I will die for your sins." He never once said, "Well, someone has to pay so it might as well be me." He knew that you were God punishing yourselves for not being good enough and he believed that if *he* took the sins of that life, that the belief in sins and punishment would cease; just as a child who believes he must be punished for something he did and asks his parent to please slap him for being a bad boy, because he did this or that wrong.

The parent with insight will know that the child is just playing a game and has done nothing wrong. The child, however, *believes* this role he is playing and asks the parent to participate. The parent sees how telling the child to not be so silly will spoil his fun, so the parent plays too and says, "Oh, don't you want me to take the slap for you?" "Of course," says the child, and is now excited because he is no longer playing this fantasy out alone. He now has a playmate who believes in his fantasy.

Let it go children. It's all just a fantasy. No pain really exists and no punishment is necessary and *no* sins exist now nor have they ever! You create what you believe to be and then you invite others to be a part of your fantasy. This one has grown, and grown, and is out of control. You beat yourselves up from inside, and soon your body gives out from all this physical abuse that is caused by judgment of yourself and others.

So far, you are just a shell of a being, and I am here to teach you how to "draw" your soul back into what was once you. You will wish to know that most souls are as confused as most humans and they don't want to return anymore than you do. This is not a subject for you to concern yourselves with. I will straighten everything out as we go. Your job is simply to continue cleaning out you so your soul can fit back in. So, go to your refrigerator and ask to receive only what is best for *your* body, and I will show you what is good and healthy and in-tune with your particular vibration.

Most of you do not know how to eat but you are very good at eating. You eat for health, you eat for energy, you eat for nourishment and most of all you eat for love. You are constantly feeding yourselves in an effort to fill up on love. Love won't come from a chocolate cake or rocky road ice cream. Love will come from the center of your being... once we can get you *into* your being or get your soul back in you.

Now; when you truly begin to see how you *are* love, you will feel good indeed. Most of what you experience now on this level is nothing as to what is available to you. You are so important to this "whole" that without just one of you the "whole" is not. It is like a giant, beautiful puzzle that has been put together over a long period of time only to have the person in charge discover a missing piece. It would never do to never find that missing piece.

So now we come to "man/woman and searching for our missing piece." Most often you do not believe you are "whole" without a love in your life. If he or she does not give you the correct amount of attention you become frustrated and begin to want more. In wanting "more" attention you create a vacuum between yourself and your intended admirer. So now he/she is not agreeing to the correct attention you deserve and so you rush at him/her with your frustration and controlling ways; and of course, he/she does not wish to be pushed so he/she now backs away before *you* push him/her away with your demands for "more."

Right now it is very difficult for most of you to "give" more than you receive. You work on a give/take basis, not a give/receive basis. You are so starved for love that you rush at anyone who looks a little "giving." When he/she does not feel that you are taking, he/she is most happy to give. You will do best to learn to sit and wait for God to deliver your own good to you. By this I do not mean that you must stay alone in a room "waiting." God will work with you and around you, and sometimes, even in spite of you. You are so vast that you are pushing parts of you away and these parts are very upset about this being pushed at, so they leave.

When he/she leaves after a good push you will know that it is simply a reflection of how you are doing inside. Male/female are "duking it out" *in* you, so you are seeing this result in your mirror. The good news for you on earth is that male/female energy is moving very rapidly into balance. All are feeling this in various stages of change. It is best described as the battle within or Armageddon or good vs. evil, or still better, positive vs. negative force; push/pull, hate/love, leave/stay, die/live, joy/anger. You are finding your balance and energy is moving rapidly into its proper place. No one feels this more than God (you). So be gentle with you and trust your own decision in all that you choose.

◈

*S*o far you are not good enough to be God. Most often you see yourselves as simply *less* than God, or God energy – or God force. This does create somewhat of a problem in showing you how God-like you actually are.

So; from now on we will discuss you as though you are royalty. Can you imagine how awkward it is to have half of my own self believing it is unworthy of the love I bestow? It is quite unlikely that you will change and begin to *receive* my love at any date in your near future. Most of you are so unhappy with how your lives are going that you cannot possibly begin to see yourselves as God.

You need to be able to blame someone for what does not work in your life. If you point the finger of judgment at your own actions, you will be calling your own self wrong. And since you are not wrong (because you do everything according to the rules *you* have laid down) you invariably suggest that your partner or the others did something wrong. This saves you face and allows your own rules to reign supreme. Once you begin to break your own rules you begin to lighten-up on others who refuse to live by these rules. When enough people on earth begin to show acceptance for each individual's *need* for following their own personal rules, we will have peace and tranquility on Mother Earth.

Most of you do not believe in government any longer and yet you continue to be *ruled* over by them. Soon this will change. Not all men are meant to be divided up into leaders and followers. There will come a time when all parts of God begin to realize the extent of life and begin to enjoy the knowledge that it is not as complicated as it all seems.

Most people on earth at this time have a great deal of awareness concerning ruling the masses. It is all based on fear at this time, and as fear leaves and light returns you will see how you are ruled only by God – *your own God-self.* It is not necessary to hold on to your *old* ways as you are now developing into a bright *new* you. I invite you all to begin to see *your* rules for what they are and not force *your* rules onto the rest of God's children. If you are silly enough to limit your own God-self with such rules, you will continue to *judge* you for every little wrong that you do. We have one big problem with this word wrong... it is not. It does not exist and not one single soul has *ever*, since creation began, done anything wrong. Right is God. God is you. You do *no* wrong, you do God's work

Now, I wish to discuss pornography. This will be difficult for you to grasp, but it is time to prepare you for Godness, not right and wrongness. First off, pornographic pictures and photographs do not necessarily project a healthy portrayal of sex and good healthy sexual intercourse. Now; don't get on your high horse here and jump to conclusions. I am not saying that there are good ways to have sexual intercourse or that there are bad ways. *Sex just is.* Just as you just are and just as I just am. We are God experimenting with matter and density. *Matter is beginning to take on spirit.* This means that you are becoming more and more God by each breath that you breathe.

Now; back to pornographic sex. So, sex is creating quite a stir on planet earth and I wish you to know that sex is good. Sex is right. Sex is God. God is sexual energy and you are sexual energy in a body. So what? You move and shake and quiver and ejaculate and climax and it feels good and your body responds as though it has been exercised and it surely has. How can you possibly be afraid of your own body, and how can you possibly think it wrong to take photographs of a body in all sorts of positions doing whatever is sexually creative?

You admire one another from afar and you create competition to show off your bodies and to exploit them in order to see how well you created you. You now have beauty competitions and exhibitions of strength and aerobics and gymnastics and wrestling and contortionism... all of this is to show off your own created form in all its glory. You may even demonstrate spitting contests, and on occasion, a few drunken students have had organized contests to show off their own endowments and what capabilities they have developed.

So; why not show off your sexual abilities? Where is the shame in showing a penis? It is no more offensive to God than your tongue or your nose. Stop being so silly and allow *all* parts of your created form to be. You were *never* told by God that any part of your own form was not to be viewed or touched or photographed. It is not my intention to upset you with this information. However, it *is* my intention to wake you up to the truth of your own fears. Your fear of sex is so great that it literally controls how you think and how you love and, especially, how you judge. Don't judge creativeness and don't judge personal choice.

Now; there is this subject of abuse which we have discussed in other books of this "Loving Light" series. One of the problems with abusive behavior is that it creates more *fear* in one or both of the participating members. Fear is what will stop you from becoming God. Nothing else stands in your way. See things as they really are, not as you have been taught to see and judge. This will do for now. I wish all of those who are reading this information to please review Book One, *God Spoke through Me to Tell You to Speak to Him* and Book Four, *The Sun and Beyond*, if you have any problem with what I have just said here. I would also like to thank Liane for allowing me to say this *my way* with no restrictions. Good day.

Now and then it is good to be human. Most often you are in a position of trying to be perfect or *what you believe to be perfect.* It is not perfect when you try. What is perfection already exists as you. You need not try to be what you already are. What you are – is me. I am God… you are God. I am love… you are love. I am faith… you are faith and I am you.

You have spent so much time trying to be your sort of perfection that you no longer let or allow all my children to grow and expand as awareness. It is not necessary to force all parts of God to rush around and be productive. It is not necessary to force them to follow a specific road in life and it is not necessary to force them to see things your way, because *your way* is simply that… *your way*.

So; for now, I would like you to remember how to be God by not doing or saying anything in particular. Just get up in the morning and do what feels good. No one ever said God must work to survive. God *is*. He does not provide for his family out of fear of lack. He *is*, just as the sky and the earth and the air that surrounds it is. The only problem with God on earth is cleaning him out so he knows he is God on earth.

❧

So often you are not certain how you feel on certain subjects. This is known as neutrality. Often you judge and take sides and this is known as separation. I am beginning to create a new and better earth based on neutrality. This new world will become… "heaven on earth."

Neutral is not bad, taking sides is not wrong, and no one ever loses. So, once I have created this new world I will sit back and observe as I have before; before you were here and before each universe was here. I put each universe in place and you are my co-creators in this particular creation. So far, not much is truly known about creation and how it works. You begin to show one another how you see it, and once you get a few to "believe" your "real" explanation, you begin to conform to what was told to you by another. You become so fearful of sounding too-far-out that you quickly control your version to fit into what is acceptable. *God is not acceptable* on earth because he is too-far-out! Most of you do not wish to sound weird so you do not get involved in far-out beliefs.

So; here is my dilemma, how do I teach you who and what I really am without losing you along the way because of weirdness or something that is just too-far-out there for you to accept? This has been a great barrier between us since time began. You are "safe" (so you believe) *in* matter and I am outside of you, and ultimately, I am outside of your belief system.

Most often *what you believe in* are rules on how to get to God or to your own personal salvation. If you were to see me as a mass of flashing lights how would you know that it was indeed me? And if those lights began to float in and out of you, your own mind, how would you perceive that as God? You are taught to look for Christ-like beings or even Satan in disguise. You are never told to *look for light.* Most often you wait for proof in the way of good deeds to show you the goodness and dispel fears concerning evil situations and trickery. So we have you all watching and judging and very skeptical.

Now I want to tell you how I will come to you. I will come as light. *Behold my light.* Do not look for good because I do not do good, *I am good.* Do not look for salvation because it *is.* And do not look for fiery displays because *I simply am.* Do not search for me outside of you because I have been admitted into matter and am now in the driver's seat. I am in you and you do not even realize how you are me. So, don't hide from God any longer. You have each been hiding and hoping for forgiveness for being so stupid, or lonely, or unconditional in your loving. You will not be forgiven by God because there is nothing to forgive.

In the true reality of God "you are perfection" and *only you* have ever doubted this perfection. You have judged others and judged God and judged actions and even reactions until I can no longer allow you to sink so *low* in the scheme of creation. Allow all to simply "be." Let go of judgment and hatred and self-righteousness. Stop pretending to be God's law enforcement team. God has *no* laws and *only* human error creates such a manipulative and controlling monster who will only love and forgive his own children at a conditional level.

This is God and I do not love and forgive. It is

not necessary to please me *ever* for *I am love* and *I am light* and I am forgiveness. I do not do these deeds of forgiving and admitting you to heaven. To imply that God forgives is to imply that I held judgment against, and I am finally allowed to call it like it is. This is a very good time for God. Not often am I allowed to be so absolutely truthful!

∾✺∾

*S*o far it is not considered wrong to be right. You each strive to be right so as not to be wrong and make a fool out of yourself. From now on I want you to let go of right and be wrong. Stop arguing with your neighbor or friend and allow right to just be. Do not "push" right on everyone else. It is not necessary to *protect* your position in life by making everyone wrong for not agreeing with you. You have been stranded here on earth for so long that you believe it is not good to be different. The only problem with your theory of conjugation is that you intend to keep everyone on the "right" track by making everyone like you!

Now; look very carefully at who and what you are and then tell me how right you are. Don't be afraid to be wrong. In your case, to be wrong is simply to be unacceptable. It is not acceptable to be insane and it is not acceptable to be talking with voices from within your own self and it is not acceptable to *be* God.

Do it your way and do not worry if they see your way as wrong. Let them do it their way and do not accept responsibility for changing how they live. In changing you, you will eventually change *everything*, as you are *all* that exists here. You simply project an image to show you how your own thoughts and beliefs are affecting creation, and this reflection comes back to you and says, "Hi, I'm so and so and I don't believe what you are doing is right!" And you jump on your high "right" horse and start to convince he or she why you believe it is best to do it your way, and in convincing he or she that *your* way is best you are actually trying to say how their way is not so good.

Leave yourself be by letting them be. So far this is creating a great imbalance for you, as you are both negative and positive vibration and you are creating both negative and positive charge as you create life in this realm. Most often you do not even know how you affect all that is, but you will. One day you will *see* how you created heaven and earth and even God. Yes, I did say you created God, not necessarily me, yet you did begin to *realize* parts of me, and in doing so *you* began to bring me to *you*. This is how creation works. You begin to realize and see and voilà, here I am – here you are and here is everything that you ever "realized" into matter.

You will begin to see me as I truly am and, in doing so, you will create an image of a more transcendable and flexible and forgivable God. You create it *all* by how you see it. *You* have the power and the ability to allow God into you and, by doing so, you allow God into matter. *God is waiting to become* and you hold the appearance of God in your hands. Dense energy does not receive – light energy receives. Please begin to *lighten* up. This is why I write in such a fashion. I am literally preparing my own way. I must enter from light vibration, and judgment is so *thick* that it is blocking entry. You must become light by being light. Stop dragging yourself and everyone else down with dense thoughts of being wrong. You do not do wrong ever and neither does *anyone* on this planet.

You must stop judgment in order to raise your own vibration and *rise* above dense energy. This is why I constantly frighten my pen by telling you how things really are. She freaks out at this information and fears being blocked by others and their inability to accept such radical change, but radical change is what has been requested and so I *give* as required to meet your needs.

⚘

*I*t has been a very long journey for you. You have left God force in order to enter matter. You do not actually leave, however the feeling is that of leaving. You changed identity by letting go of your "idea" of who and what you are. You left home by changing your mind about reality and now I want you to return by changing back to who you are. By most peoples own admission they are not what they seem. They are much, much more. I want you to reconsider your point of view; change your mind and change you. You are God and when you begin to see God in all, you will see God in your own mirror.

So far, not one of you is willing to change. It is good to know who you are and the most difficult part of transition is to change. You are each God in transition; God is in change. God went numb and blind and dumb in order to create density and matter. Matter has a very dense vibration and in order to "fit in" God changed his molecular and atomic and energy structure. So now God has changed and rebuilt and redefined himself in order to "be" part of created matter, and he must now reverse what he is. He must begin to spin in the opposite direction in order to reverse dense vibration into "light" vibration and become God or this Second Coming.

It is best to allow all to reverse at their own rate. Some are spun out into matter at such a dense level that I may become responsible for their safety myself. This has not yet been decided. Each of you has free will and each of you decides when you wish to become God inside matter or creation. When those who have buried their light so deep in matter decide that this is enough, I will be here to assist. I do not come to aid only those who are ready and I do not decide who is ready and who is not. I simply check in on each of you to see how you are doing "in" created matter.

Liane and others have been screaming to get out or get unstuck for some time. She chose to reverse and "feel" the reverse or the pull-out or de-materialization. Hence, she has seen her life change drastically as she has re-entered light and left huge amounts of darkness behind. Along with her "hold" on matter has gone her matter or "material security."

I have asked Liane to "hold" nothing but God. I ask her repeatedly to let go of all and allow God to run her show – her life. She has been very good in giving up and I am happy she has chosen such an extreme but peaceful way back to God. I say peaceful because she has fought and kicked and screamed most of the way back out of dense matter. But she did come willingly and she has enough peace and calm in her life to represent a gift and she still wants more.

So as long as she wants more I will continue to work with her to bring her out! Out of fear, out of misery, out of poor health, out of lack of love and into the light of God.

To change back to God light is not easy from where you sit. It is actually the simplest of all change, but your fear of losing is so great and your fear of harm and danger is overwhelming you. Look danger in the eye and see fear for what it is. It is not pain, it is belief. Stop believing *in* fear and begin to rise above it and out of it. It is a very big weight that is holding you down and out of God. You never left God, yet you created a "belief" that you did and that belief in separation is very, very powerful. *Let it go!*

≈≈≈

For such a long time it has been undesirable to be with you. God is not permitted to walk with you.

You have cut God off. You have left God out. Now I come to you as one of you and through one of you and this will not be acceptable for some time.

You see; you need love on this planet. If you had love you would not refuse to see me as you. Love is not what you make it out to be. Of course, most of what you see is so distorted and upside down from your view point. You don't even know where you fit in so how can you possibly see God and how he fits in? So, most of what you now believe is not what is.

I will now tell you a story about love. You will like this. So far I have not put you down and I have not made you look bad and I have not gotten upset, or angry with your ignorance and lack of trust and even your failure to co-operate with me. This is all part of love. Love is accepting and allowing and not hurting, or hitting, or shooting. The reason I tell you not to kill is out of a desire to protect you from you. You kill and you begin to see anger and hatred and pain and guilt and I want you to see love. So I say, "Do not kill" – not you, not them and not any.

Then I ask you not to love any before your own self. This is to assure that you put you first. When you put others before your own idea of self you are creating separation, and this separation is just as real as separation caused by saying "I am better than they are."

So now I am justifying my teachings to you and I do this in order to help you see how it is not necessarily easy to show you who you are and how you handle life.

Now, I wish to discuss drugs and this problem you have with addiction. Stop telling others how to live their lives. It is enough for you to clear this you, and when you get all riled up and begin preaching life and death choices to others you become more fearful and more dense. Stop pushing them to change because in doing so you are creating more problems for you.

So; now, we have you all sitting around and doing nothing out of fear of doing the wrong thing. Don't worry. You will always know when something is not so good for you. That is, once I clean you out you will know. Most of you are buried so deep in matter and dense emotion that you no longer "feel" what is good for you. You have lost your will to live and now simply struggle against death and dying and any loss. So far you do not look so good, and of course you cannot see this as you are "stuck" in matter and cannot find your way out. So, I am sending you messages to remind you where you are and how to return by developing your own intuition once again. Now, how can you develop intuition when you are drugged on stimulants and depressants?

✥

*S*o now you are beginning to see how it is indeed much more to live than simply by human terms. So far there is a great deal of human information that is incorrect and yet other information that requires great clarification.

Sometimes it becomes difficult to enlighten on this plane. This, we believe, is due to the complications incurred at entrance. Most often you are so tied into your own belief in what is, that you forget to acknowledge the *idea* of separation and change and growth. If indeed a single vibratory spark is capable of ignition on this plane it is also available on others. So; if I began to write through this woman and ignite the spark that awakens "like souls," I also am capable and even likely to demonstrate such a connection in other time continuums. Once I begin to invade space with my presence, I am allowed *time*. Time does not exist in reality; however, you are not in reality so therefore you use time as an equivalent to measure space elapsed.

Now; when I began to *erupt* into matter, I did so as a way of becoming myself or more of Godliness. Godliness is space/time/thought and much more. Nothing is God because God is all; therefore God is nothing as well as everything. Most often what is believed to be matter is in reality *nothing*. Matter does not exist as a substitute for spirit. Matter was put in place to show you how you might be if you were not spirit or God. What if??? – That is the name of this game. What if – instead of this I did this? What if – instead of matter I chose spirit? What if – instead of spirit I chose dense matter, or even solid matter? What if – I chose life instead of death and death over life as it is now known? What if – life *is* the unconscious death of spirit? And what if – spirit exists as life in what is now called death?

It is not so important to live in life that is not conducive to spirit. If life is not good it is pain. Life that is pain is not death but it is not good for spirit. Life is to be lived. Spirit lives regardless of form. Form *will* learn to accommodate spirit more fully in order to ascend to a level of balance. Balance will be achieved through love and love will be achieved through *acceptance* that God is you and you are God. Many people will die in order to live.

So far it has been a very good part of you that realizes your potential. Most often you do not realize how vast yet segregated you have grown. It is almost like a line waiting to buy concert tickets. The people closest to the ticket office still remember why they have come and they are spreading the word back to those who are simply standing in line taking up space. Those to the end have completely lost it and are arguing and fighting over who is in front of who. The silliest part of this is that they don't even remember what show they came to view or how long they were told it would take them to become admitted to this fine show.

So; as this confusion grows and they wait and fight, they also begin to "wonder" why they are here and what keeps them from leaving. Some of you have begun to leave the end of this line and no longer wait for admittance into such a fine show. After all, why wait in a long line if you don't know what in the world it's for? This has become your way out of line and it is through death or suicide that you leave.

Do not judge those who choose to abandon ship or check out of line. *It is not a sin to kill yourself.* Now, I do not wish you to go berserk or off the deep end on this topic. I am simply saying that you are God and you created you and you can do whatever you wish with what *you have created.*

You have a great deal to learn and most of what is meant as truth has been distorted and changed to protect your very sensitive and fragile *ego*. Ego is fear. Ego was once God awareness who did not complete his cycle of evolution. He became stuck in fear and has been lying to you ever since.

Ego is afraid. He is afraid of life because he may end. It is as though he were afraid to walk because he may fall and break a leg. Therefore… ego blocks you from living. He says, "No, this is bad," or "That is wrong." And of course, since all of you have graduated through six grades of God's truth and are now in my seventh grade class, you all *know* how right-and-wrong/good-and-bad are simply distorted beliefs. Mostly I want you to know that you can come or go, live or die, stay or leave. It *is* your choice.

Now, so far you have no wish to discuss your love life in public. It turns you off and even disgusts most of you to hear specifics on this daily function. And of course now, with the AIDS scare or fear, you have a real good excuse to shut down and not function. It doesn't really matter you know? Nothing you do changes what you are. You may cry and scream and hide in your fears, but I know and you know that *you are God*.

So, let's see you try to get out of that one. You can't and you know it. So, let's give all the other Gods a break and not push them out of line or tell them how or where they must stand. You don't even know why you're here so stop pretending to.

So far it has been expressed on earth that to love is painful and to die is worse. You are so very confused on these two issues. To love is not pain and to die is to emerge from a cocoon of ignorance into a conscious state of semi-awareness.

Not everyone is meant to be on earth. That is correct. Even once in a great while a true soul takes a wrong turn and ends up in never-never land; never do this and never do that and if you do, make certain you don't get caught. Yes, this *is* never-never land.

So you begin to ask how to get back to your right place, and in "asking," you will be shown your own particular path home. And if this path should guide you to me this too is most enjoyable. You see; you will only know me by knowing yourself and to know you is to love you. So I have decided that it is best to help you up and out of this dense layer of belief programming concerning death, pain, love and exhaustion of living.

You are so caught up in fear of pain and fear of death that you are tired – tired of life and tired of being you. How can I possibly get you to love your own self when you don't like you? You judge yourself at every turn, and if you do not someone else will. This is what you have created in order to keep you in line. Do not do this and do not do that. This is never-never land and it is killing you. You are damned if you do and damned if you don't. Strike a blow and you save a child from abuse, and with that same blow you are now the abuser.

How did you get so *wound up* in all this red tape and democracy and lunacy? I will explain. You began to make rules out of fear of losing control. The more rules – the less control you wielded. Give someone else power, and in doing so, give that same person *responsibility*. Do you see how you created this two headed monster that literally feeds you with new fear ideas in order to keep you in line? *Fear is out of control*, it is not running this planet because it does not belong here and it is searching for its proper place, as are you.

Fear is basically your own inability to love your own self. The least little anxiety is fear and self-love turned to self-hatred. It is insecure and vulnerable; and it is anger. You know fear well. You sell and purchase antacid and pain relievers and ulcer cures and stress control ideas. The stress is fear. The acid in your stomach is created by the digestive tract that is out of whack due to intense nervous response to living in a constant state of panic. You do not need a headache pill; you need a good dose of *love*. Love will cure all and love will give you back you.

When you can learn to love without control, you will truly be in the driver's seat of your own vehicle. This vehicle was chosen by you because it best suited your particular purpose in this particular life. Treat your body as well as you would treat a brand new, shiny, expensive car. Don't park in dangerous areas. Don't take in bad fuel and please clean out your engine and carburetor once a day to run smoothly. Enema is a very good system to use and I highly suggest you begin soon. It's not such a great dinner topic, but in a few years you will be well on your way to ascension; and who will even remember what you did to get to complete *inner* awareness.

It is so simple. *You are what you put in you.* Stop putting in what doesn't work *for* you. Begin to clean out you and your cells will reproduce as never before and you will begin to remember who you are. It is energy that runs you. You are energy. Food goes in and turns to fuel energy. Energy is what runs your body and you will not unclog your valves long enough to get your own cells reproducing. And what do cells carry? *Information!!!*

Cellular memory is stored *in* you. You do not need to search outside of your own self. You have the information of this created universe and much, much more right inside of little ol' you. Imagine that! You are God on two legs and you are so blind and confused that you won't even believe it when you're told. Not too clear, are you? Well, this too shall pass. Soon you will begin to clear, and create, at such a rate that you will astound even your own self into believing just a little bit of this big truth.

You are asleep, you are unconscious, and now you are reading in order to know who and what you are. A bird does not find it necessary to know he is a bird before he will fly. He simply flies instinctively. Well, the problem here my children, is that you no longer remember how to fly by instinct. Instinct is buried. It is dead and gone. You replaced instinct and trust with rules and punishment for not following. So; now we have many who no longer choose to follow and this is very, very good.

☙❧

*I*t has not been so long ago that you each

decided to leave and do your own thing so to speak. You did not wish to be held in place by a punishing God so you left me!

Now – I am totally aware of the fact that I have explained for you in our fourth book that I pushed at you in order to move you from my presence. No one ever gets the boot without requesting, in some way, to be moved on. So you now play the victim quite often when the truth is you are asking to be moved or shoved or pushed. You believe that you are rejected and left alone, but in truth you are asking to be left alone and you are asking to be pushed, because you are "stuck" in a particular area and you wish to move on and leave your attachments and addictions-to behind.

So far you are all screaming out that no one loves you, and you are simply seeing how no one but you even questions that you are of importance enough to live. You are being focused into one small area of belief in order to show how you are "stuck" in this material realm. If I were to take you outside of yourself and show you how you look to me, you would see how you are attached to pain in certain areas of your existence and this attachment to pain creates pain.

So what is occurring at this moment in time is a form of focus, or narrowing down to see. Envision, if you will, a funnel that allows you to see only a specific area where pain is attached to you. With this funnel vision you are capable of seeing a big over-all view that gets smaller and smaller as you focus in on the specific area of your being where you hold pain. This area is now being activated in order for you to see and look at pain. If I were to allow you to continue pretending that you have no pain, you would eventually create death and no longer be a part of ascension.

So; most of you are in confusion and pain because God wants you to look into your problems and hurts. To ignore you is to push you from you. I wish you to "open" to love and open to you. Do not be afraid to see who you are and how you got to be you. You are coated and layered with experience and now is the time to look closely at your own layers and camouflage. You have hidden your true identity and I wish for you to come forward out of your hiding place.

You are so confused about pain that you have begun to judge yourself for creating this pain. When you learn how you manipulated energies in order to survive in matter you will no longer judge pain. Do you know that without pain you would allow a broken bone to go untreated and continue to abuse that area of your body? *With* pain you say, "Ouch, I hurt this and must be gentle with myself until I heal." Maybe pain is actually very good for you and you forgot how to use it, so now you judge it. Use your powers wisely. Listen to your body. Listen to your mind, and especially listen to your heart. Your heart is the domain for peace. Through your heart you will know self-love which is *all* that I require in order to come into my own body.

God has created form and now he wishes to enter. Stop blocking God's birth by judging yourself. When you are God it is okay to acknowledge your own magnificence. Go in peace and love yourself from top to bottom and from past to present and from outside in. I do!

God

✿

*I*t is not such a good idea to treat you like children. You are so unnerved by anyone who assumes you to not know everything that you scream in defense of your knowledge. Most of you are so dense and so lonely and so confused that, were I to say to you face to face that you suffer from loneliness, you would quickly reassure me of your popularity and numbers that support this belief in community and family love.

You are not afraid to be alone; however you are afraid to be lonely. You hold on to others for safety and you actually verbalize your "need" for them. It's not only unsafe for you it's 'unsure' for you. You feel ill at ease when someone doesn't agree with you and you struggle to be accepted. When, in actuality, in being accepted you are conforming to another's wish for you. In being you, you are staying alone or in your right place.

So far you are not certain who you are, so you do not feel it important to be isolated or alone. As you grow in awareness you begin to "see" how separation began, and in seeing how separation began you too may wish to separate. It is not wrong to separate yourself from church, from state, from country, from family or from your friends. You are seeing how you came here and reviewing the path you took.

When you arrived on this plane you began a very long separation process that began with energy and continued on in form. So far it is not the process that created pain. The process was simply a way of becoming "more" by separating into multi-levels and multi-dimensions. It's this process that will call to you to begin to leave those you most want to be connected with. These are your soul mates and as you move back in time and retrace the steps that brought you here, you will see how recollecting your past is actually a way of finding a better way to live.

When you began to play with energy you began to create many possibilities. One of these possibilities is located inside your own self. You carry within you a total bank of knowledge and information that is based on how you receive it. When you begin to uncover who you are, you begin to destroy your cover or discard it. No more hiding in darkness and pretending you are not light. You are so buried that we have a great deal of digging at hand. So; when you begin to cop to the light or the truth, you begin to hurt. Your layers of density are peeled away and you often must change your viewpoint or position in thinking. All this changing and position shifting becomes quite uncomfortable and quite often you will wish to stop seeing truth.

It is not that you do not wish to complete this layering business; it is simply that you have seen enough and wish to stop looking through the looking glass. When you come to this point you may wish to rest and leave the work to God. I do not expect you to do this work, and you are simply responding to my process of self-restoration in working on your own restoration. Everything is handed down from the father and everyone is the father. So; when the father wishes to clear he sends signals to his body to request clearing. He is listened to often, and in areas where he cannot receive proper attention, he will find a new way to send the signal for love and self-preservation.

So; as you clear, you begin to raise your level of consciousness and in raising this level of consciousness you begin to let go of fear. Fear is the line that *connects* you to this material plane. Fear of lack and loss are great and you all wish to keep friends and lovers and cars and houses and jewelry because it *marks* you. It says to this dimension, "here is a fine person. He or she created wealth because he or she believes in love of self." The only catch here is that he or she does not love self and actually created the golden calf out of fear of not having or fear of loss.

As you go along in this business of returning to God I wish you to remember one thing. It is okay to have material wealth when it is flowing in and out of your life like life force energy. When you begin to cling to and cherish wealth you are beginning to block its flow. Start loving you with energy and energy will flow to you.

One of the reasons I do not speak often of money is to keep you interested in returning to me. When I begin to say that your value to me has nothing to do with possessions, you get very nervous and fearful that you will become a vagabond with no possessions. Why does that thought frighten you so much? Do you perhaps believe that those who have less *are* less? Or maybe you believe that those who have less are going to struggle and suffer. I see many on your planet who suffer and struggle and this struggle is to *get more*. If they were to let go of this struggle for more they just may see an improvement in their mentality and maybe even "peace of mind." It is very difficult to be God (which is spirit) when you are carrying a big load of gold (which is heavy and material). Let it go... it is truly not important. Make what you will of this writing, but this is the *truth* of it.

❧

*M*ost of you feel that you are not worthy of life as you now know it. You believe that you are not allowed to fully express your true intent, and you also see pain in all that occurs around you most often. You are not aware that pain exists in your life. You live your life with gusto or you live your life with simplicity and you cannot understand why you get a headache or an ulcer or heartburn or hair fall-out. It is all caused by pain; pain in the form of mistrust and misunderstanding and even misuse of your power to assimilate what you have seen or experienced.

Most of you are aware that *you do not agree with change.* It is much more comfortable for you to stay as you are because where you are is tested and tried and accepted already. To accept a new style of living that is not an upgrade would seem most uncomfortable to you because it would mean great change and fear of loss or lack. Most often loss or lack is followed by stress and depression. Why is this? Why do you *believe* that this world is contingent on how you want your car to look or how you want your home to look or even how you want to look to others? This is ego at work. Ego has taken over and I wish you to get off your ego high horse and begin to flow into change whether it looks good to you or not.

You will return to God as a disassembled body form and there will be no room in your pockets for wealth you have accumulated on planet earth. You may scrimp and save and possess with the best of them, but it does you no service in heaven. Wealth on this level must remain on this level. Think of it as working as hard as you can your entire life simply to leave it behind for others.

Now; if this be your choice, I suggest you begin to enjoy giving it to those who need it now. Don't wait to die and allow *your* legal system to eat away at your dream for others. Others (you) are in need of food and housing now. So I suggest, if you plan on working hard for a living, you do it with full awareness that *it* is not yours to keep. You are here playing *in* matter and you are confused into thinking you own it. You do not! No one owns. This is a very big illusion. You do not own your property. You are simply being allowed to use what is here.

To hoard money and property is really very silly to see. It is like hoarding the pieces of a chess game so you won't lose the game. So, now I have upset many who believe *in* prosperity. What I wish you to do with your wealth is play. Play with what you have and do not give it any importance. It *is* yours as long as you wish to *hold* on to it. Just remember, if you hold on to the chess pieces, you will never experience moving them into a winning position. How can you win if you won't *let go* of the very stuff that creates the game. You are here to *play* the game not to become attached to it.

So, my final word on wealth is to say that when I speak of your prosperity it has little if anything to do with money. Prosperity is a way of seeing absolutely everything that occurs in your life. You may hold on to your stuff or you may let go of your stuff. It really doesn't matter. Nothing that you do here on earth is going to stop the Second Coming. The Second Coming, as you all know from our previous books, is simply *you* becoming God. God is waking up and he will not *need* wealth. God needs only love and even that is a misstatement of the facts. God *is* love, but has *forgotten* that this is his true identity.

You will wish to let go of this false identity so God can awaken *within* your consciousness. God is ready to be born and you, my dear sweet child, are part of this vast womb that will carry and nurture the very seed that is life itself. Rejoice children of this planet. You may be asked to let go of your possessions but you will *receive* the greatest of all gifts for your part in creating God. Yes; God is now, was then, and always will be. And now he is even, ever more. He is all… you are all. You are "becoming" God.

❧

So far it has been a most enjoyable experience to actually control matter by writing through one of my own cells. Mostly it is a case of "knowing" how to use my own will in the three dimensional world. It is often said that to know you is to love you and that is exactly how I arrive on earth. As you each begin to know who you are, you begin to take on new dimension and expand into a new fulfilled self. Each time I show you something new you *become* a little new. Knowledge is what you are and to know your own self is not so good in your eyes.

Most of you have childhood trauma and even adult trauma that you chose to forget. In forgetting, you are literally blocking your flow of energy. All energy is meant to flow to the left and around to the right. It was never meant to block on the left and never make it back to the right. Right hand gives out and left hand receives. You however, have been receiving with your right and so we see a very materialistic and socially corrupt society. Most often what you think you are creating is a giant prosperous society. The truth is that in order to receive properly you must remove *aggression* from your daily lives. Aggression is simply a way of pushing *out* and becoming stronger. "The bigger, the better" is the motto for aggressiveness. Stay small and simple is my motto.

If I were to expand on my left to fill the void that is now there I would not *become* for some time. In order for God to become I must first be created. To be created I must begin as idea and rush *toward* this planet, sort of like a projection sent forth. After I have rushed into position I must *hold on* and germinate. To hold on I must be attached in some way. In the same way that plant life often clings to a wall I cling to matter in order to be part of creation *as you see it*. Not all of creation is as you see it; however the problem here is not to see what you see, but to *become* what you see.

I do not become you out of a desire to be accepted by you. I become you out of a desire to be held in your realm by you. You are so busy running in and out of this dimension that you don't always *see* me when you leave. You have forgotten how you came to be. You have forgotten your job. You no longer remember why you went to your place of work. You went to create a vision. This vision is God and God is waiting for his co-workers to show him the way in. Don't forget any longer. Wake up. Begin to remember. Begin to take *on* light! Live only in awareness and show me my way in. It is very dark and I need both direction and guidance upon my entry. I am coming in to visit and I wish to know that you *receive* me.

In order to receive you must begin to turn on your left lobe to assist your right. Right lobe gives out signals that say, "You are God. You are love. You are here to receive God's entry." Left lobe sends out signals that say, "I am perfect and must continue to be perfect or I will be lost. Don't let go. Hang on to all sinking ships at all costs for we must not lose." Something like this is what's going on *in* you at this point in time. You will not be lost if you give up and give in. To give up and give in is indeed how you will learn to *receive*. You do not receive by holding on to. God is the one who must hold on to you and you must give up to God.

⁂

*I*t is not often that you are truly honest and show you who you are. You are so very multifaceted that you could literally become many individuals all at once. You are very, very independent of your other selves and often you are totally unaware how you are in control of them as well as this you. You – this very unconscious identity is so full of lives that they are screaming for your attention.

You have the ability to stay projected *within* matter and to *totally* ignore all other parts of your own self. It is as though you projected your entire image or identity into a single cell within your body and then said "There, this is it! I am all that I am!" And of course, what you are has only a fragment to do with this one isolated lonely cell.

You are all that could possibly exist and now you are going to *know* it! You will become more of you by seeing how you are actually all that is. It is time to wake up! This is it! The Second Coming is at hand and many are confused and going through great change. Change will allow you to see more clearly how life is not as you believe. Life is God. God is all. All is you.

You have a very big job to do and you are the one who you trust to do this work. When you pray to God, you literally pray to your own identity. You are the creator; the chosen one; the Second Coming of God is *you* telling others and yourself that you have successfully "*become*" through denseness and darkness. The salvation of life is met in death – death of the old and birth of the true you. Lay down your arms. Stop arguing to be right and begin to know you are the king of light. You dozed off to see how it would feel to go under. Now you are coming to know you are God, and you will know who you became in order to lose God.

You left for a purpose and now your mission is near completion. Many are beginning to *know* and to ask why and this is good. It has not been so long as you believe. You started this as a way of becoming more and gaining "insight" into self. This is God speaking to his own self. I am asking each of you to communicate with me in order to heal me. Pain became a deterrent and now we must *release all pain from our subconscious memory.*

So far you are not in the mood to "look at"

pain. You wish to hold on to old patterns and adapt new ways to deal with situations all in order to not change. If you choose change it is mandatory to let go of the old. Stop holding on! Now; there are those who wish to stop pain by becoming part of it. These are the victims of disease and big practical reasons for staying *in* pain. One reason may be to accommodate a patient who is an invalid or in a wheelchair. So; pain says, "Oh, I must assist this person and suffer right along with him or her as it is good and right to do so."

Fine! Now you get to *share* in his or her anguish. What you claim as yours becomes yours. So, I suggest you begin to assist others by letting *them* keep their own pain. It is of no service to you and your own waking up process to be struggling to overcome a lesson that is not yours. Take responsibility for *you* not for he or she who has become a burden. God will care for each individual on this planet, and to die is not bad so let go of this fear of letting others go. They do not belong here and you are making a big mistake in assuming that *you* are responsible for them. I know that this is most difficult for you to understand at this point in your healing. Life is for living and death is for changing! Allow death to be and go on about your own business. Stop strangling "life" by holding it so tightly.

☙❧

*I*t is a very difficult time for you now. Most often you struggle with your own identity and how you will present *your* truth to this planet. It is not long ago that you decided to become matter in order to expand God consciousness. Most of you do not remember how it felt before this material plane existed. It was a most enjoyable time for God. I did not involve myself so much with future endeavors nor did I deem it necessary to control nature and her course.

It is only after the fall that I began to take a controlling interest in how you would *receive* me. You became so blind to all aspects of your true self that I deemed it necessary to step in and wake you up a bit. It's not such a good idea to have dense energy accumulating around my spirits and them totally unconscious to this fact. So, I decided to step in and shake you a bit to let you *know* that you are God.

One of the ways I decided to educate you was by messenger, and of course you got his message a little confused and I have decided that it's not such a good idea to send another messenger. Somehow you like to follow the leader and this causes great confusion. The more independent you are – the greater your vibratory field of expulsion. Once you become *like* others you begin to meld into their vibratory field. It is most important to remain free in order to join God.

Most of you do not wish to think for yourself so you buy into common beliefs and even hypocrisy, only because it is being given the greatest power by others. So, if fear prevails in *their* eyes you begin to buy into fear. If love prevails you buy into love. The greatest problem at this point is the absence of trust and faith. Everyone spouts the bible and its great teachings but no one is ready to look for God. It is as if you do not trust anything unless someone writes it down for you. You believe what is untrue because someone made a mistake over two thousand years ago and they *thought* what they wrote was correct and even went so far as to justify its correctness.

Now I have thousands of my cells calling themselves Christian and believing that they are the true children of God because they read a book and believed what it said. They *are* the true children of God and so are you. Absolutely everyone on this planet was created and given life by God. No one else is here. It is *all* God. So, please stop preaching that some make it to heaven and some do not. You are no closer to the truth of God than those who worship calves and other artifacts.

Don't you get it? Time has left you behind. You are preaching and shouting fear. Why teach fear when you are love? God does not punish. God is not a vengeful being and God wants only to clear up this mistaken impression of myself. If you continue to preach and teach separateness I will begin to save you from your own self. This is how much love I have for you. Jesus did not die on a cross for your sins. Jesus died simply to show you who you are and how death does *not* exist.

If you allow this simple teaching to control your life you are making God out to be a bigot who only will forgive under certain conditions. I am no bigot and I forgive all before they begin to sin, by allowing them free will. Why on earth would a loving unconditional God create spirits, give them free will and then punish them for using that free will?

Begin to *see* what is happening here. Stop pretending to believe such nonsense about God. I love you all unconditionally with no stipulations whatsoever. If you cannot deal with this simple fact then you are creating fear of God. I do not wish to be presumptuous in my findings; however I do wish *fear of God* to cease to exist. Be careful how you see me for I am the light of this world, I am not its executioner. If you believe in death and destruction by God's wrath you are mistaken.

This is not the true God. God is love – not hate and anger. So, I hope this helps you to see who you are and even how you too may *fall* into worshiping false Gods.

*I*t is not such a good idea to push at you. You are in a state of fluxation, a state of movement, change and evolution. Once you begin to slow down and smell the roses you will become a workable instrument for God. God does not wish to impose, however it is most necessary that you stop being so material and become spirit. God is being born *in* you and to *hold* his greatness is a very big job.

So; for those who feel like getting out of the rat race and jumping on God's bandwagon, you are most appreciated. It will be difficult to break from tradition and honor and objectivity, but mine is not an objectivity oriented type of coming. My coming is spirit based and love oriented. It requires no leads to a better paying job, no goal orientation and no goal programming. It requires only *love*.

God does not work as man would like and God does not work for man. Man is God and man works to *become* God in matter. So; if your job here is to become God and your goal is to be rich, how can you possibly attain each reward? It is not a time of duality so much as it is a time of change. You are each changing for God. You lose your job and you choose another way to pay your bills, when you could simply put your faith in God and do what *you* want and not what is required in order to gain wealth.

Now, the problem we have created here is how to attain wealth without *holding* on to it. It, as all, is energy and is meant to flow. So if you *hold* money it blocks energy flowing into your life. Look at it this way; you only have two hands and if both are full of money, how do you hold love or peace of mind or any of my other gifts. Most of you believe that to be wealthy is the ultimate reward on this planet. You judge those who do not have it as being less capable of creating good for themselves. You even go so far as to judge them as not desirable. They are too poor for your social circle or not rich enough to marry your child. Money is the true God that you worship at this time. A God form, or God head is simply the deity that you pay most attention to… money is it here on earth!

*S*o, now I have you each wondering how you will care for your loved ones and who will care for you. Mostly I wish to dispel any belief in karmic responsibility. This is not how you were meant to function. Most often you create a belief system to *protect* yourself from yourself.

In the beginning you began to *believe* that you could do no wrong. So you created happily and joyously and even painlessly. You began to *open* new frontiers of exploration for others to follow, and in doing so you created roads or pathways into creation. You began to take on the role of leader and head council for those who followed. So; when you turned back to those who followed you and said "It's dark in this direction" or, "It's dangerous out here," they bought into *your* belief and passed the word back to the rest of the exploring spirits. Much in the same way that a wagon train in the old west could blaze a trail you were blazing a trail.

Now; if we look closely at this type of exploration, we will see that not always did the leader know the whole picture. Now that you have availability of aerospace technology you can see how other methods and techniques could have made this entire wagon train adventure less of an ordeal. However, we are where we are and this is how we learn. My job is not to point out mistakes and punish as you are often taught. My job is to show you a *better* way.

There are many, many, many paths to God. All have a purpose. All exist. All are logical to open minds and all are acceptable. However, what if God looked down smiled at you and said "Hi there, I see the big *picture* and I want to show you how to do it right now; not later, not sooner, but right now." And of course, since I see the big picture I also see how you can be fooled and tricked by your own fear.

So, I ask you each to begin to look at a simpler easy way of solving this big problem you have created around good and bad, i.e., good people go to heaven, bad ones do not. This is so completely off base that I wish it were possible to show you now how this confusion all came about. But for now I will just share with those who are waking from this bad guy/good guy belief system. It is so totally out of character for God to call part of his self bad or good. No one is bad or good. *All are.*

⁂

*I*t is not good to be so bad to you. You are so accustomed to treating yourself with loathsome attitudes that you no longer find the good in you. You are God and along the way you forgot you are God and began to accuse yourself of being awful for this or that mistake, or terrible for lying and cheating, or just plain wrong for all your decisions. Most of you have such low self-esteem programmed into you that you are frequently mistrustful and even downright hateful. So, the more you believe yourself to be hateful and unloving the more hate filled and unloving you become.

Now is a very strange time for most of you. You are beginning to see how you are God and yet you are being shown how you are not so God-like. The problem with this theory is simple enough. God cannot *not* be God. God can only evolve *through* his own creation and his creation *is* him.

So, to be human is the epitome of being God. To make mistakes is not wrong and to make silly choices is your rightful expression of human self. Do not beat yourself up for making a choice that later "looks" stupid. It's just God playing in matter and learning as he experiments. I never meant for you to get so hung up on right and wrong, or good vs. bad. Let these beliefs go. Be good by simply letting you and your decisions be.

Now, I wish to discuss death. You are not so afraid of death as you are afraid of pain. Pain you know, death you fear because you do not know it in this life. Life has become painful and death has become a door out of pain. It is okay to die. It is okay to live. It is okay to be God and live, or die as you choose. So be it!

❧

Once in a great while I begin to arrive on earth. It is not so much a joy at this point. It is painful to most who *receive* my vibration. This pain is experienced through cellular triggers that are in place to receive light. Light was once all that was. Then we began to include darkness and all of its vibrations. So far, earth is but a flicker of light and mostly dark. This is not a doomsday report. This is simply what is.

You have so much pain on this level that it creates confusion and fear. We also have *belief* in death which creates great amounts of judgment. Most often judgment is seen as pain, in that "judgment lowers your body's temperature enough to slow it down." Most of what you judge has to do with living and dying or truth and lying. For example: you do not die, so I say don't worry if you kill someone. Now I have created greater fear by truth. Truth frightens you to the extent that you live a lie. You are a lie. You even judge what you are as not good enough. You wish for *more* and *better* and *happier,* when in actuality, you have more and better and happier right now. So, why can't you *see* what you are and what you have? This is a good place to end and start again.

I am ending this book to allow you time; time to think, time to love and time to raise your vibration. I will write another book soon and I will call it *God's Imagination.*

For now, I wish you to *think* hard and long about the *truth* and why you fear truth. Come home to God and know that I am *all* that exists. If evil exists in you eyes, it is my evil. Whatever *you* create by your *imagination* belongs to God. You are God. Stop hiding from who you are and stop romancing this notion that you have nothing to do with creation as it now exists. You created *all* that you see and *all* that you are hiding from. You are simply a frightened child who began to believe in its own dreams and fantasies. You are no longer dreaming subtle fantasies and I am now waking you out of this nightmare.

No death ever happens! Not ever… stop blaming them for killing and stop blaming yourself for watching. Let it be….

God

God's Pen

I first heard the voice of God in 1988. I was sitting in my back yard reading a book when this big booming voice interrupted with, "I am God and I will not come to you by any other name." I felt like the voice was everywhere – inside of me as well as in the sky around me. I was so frightened that I ran in my bedroom to hide.

This was not the first time that I heard voices. I had been communicating with my own spirit guide or soul for about a year. I guess my depth of fear regarding God, and all that he represented to me at the time, was just too much.

I spent two days trying to avoid the voice of God, which was patiently waiting for me to respond. By the second day I was exhausted from lack of sleep and decided to give in and talk with him. This turned out to be the greatest gift and best decision of my life.

The first book, *God Spoke through Me to Tell You to Speak to Him*, shows my evolution from communicating with my soul to communicating with the Big Guy. It took a couple years for me to be comfortable communicating with God. My fear of a punishing God was big! That has most definitely changed and I now think of God as my partner and best friend.

In the beginning the voice of God would wake me in the middle of the night and tell me it was time to write. He said I had promised to do this work (I assumed he was talking about the soul/spirit me). I would drag myself up to a sitting position and watch in amazement as my hand flew across the page, while I tried to keep up by reading what was being written.

It was always so much fun to wake up the next morning and grab my notebook to see what God had written during the night. After some time the voice stopped waking me and I became comfortable picking up my pen and writing for God first thing in the morning. I think in the beginning I had to be awakened while still semi-conscious from sleep so I wouldn't object too much to the information that was being channeled through me.

As I grew less and less afraid (and more trusting) of God, he was able to communicate greater information. Some of the information is quit controversial, but I felt it important to just let it be and not censor it. I present the writings here to you as they were given to me. I have edited a little (mostly the more personal information regarding myself) and I have used a pen name for privacy reasons. I asked God for a good pen name and he guided me to Liane which (I was told) in Hebrew means "God has answered."

At one point I became a little concerned about my sanity in all this, so I went to a hypnotherapist to find out what I was doing. Under hypnosis I saw this incredibly huge beam of light with a voice coming from within it. It was a giant "loving light" and felt so comforting and kind. It felt like that's where I came from. After that I stopped worrying about my sanity. If this is crazy, I think it's a very good kind of crazy to be....

In loving light, Liane

Loving Light Books

Available at:
Loving Light Books: www.lovinglightbooks.com
Amazon: www.amazon.com
Barnes & Noble: www.barnesandnoble.com

Also Available on Request at Local Bookstores

www.ingramcontent.com/pod-product-compliance
Lightning Source LLC
LaVergne TN
LVHW011358080426
835511LV00005B/337